Dress Design...

Talbot Hughes

THE ARTISTIC CRAFTS SERIES
OF TECHNICAL HANDBOOKS
EDITED BY W. R. LETHABY

DRESS DESIGN

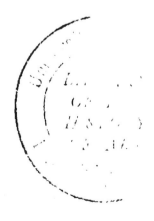

A Long-trained Muslin Dress.   About 1800.

DRESS DESIGN

AN ACCOUNT OF COSTUME
FOR ARTISTS & DRESSMAKERS
BY TALBOT HUGHES · ILLUS-
TRATED BY THE AUTHOR FROM
OLD EXAMPLES · TOGETHER
WITH 35 PAGES OF HALF-TONE
ILLUSTRATIONS

LONDON
SIR ISAAC PITMAN & SONS, LTD.
BATH, MELBOURNE, TORONTO, AND NEW YORK

Reprinted 1920

GENERAL PREFACE TO THE SERIES

IN issuing this volume of a series of Handbooks on the Artistic Crafts, it will be well to state what are our general aims.

In the first place, we wish to provide trustworthy text-books of workshop practice, from the points of view of experts who have critically examined the methods current in the shops, and putting aside vain survivals, are prepared to say what is good workmanship, and to set up a standard of quality in the crafts which are more especially associated with design. Secondly, in doing this, we hope to treat design itself as an essential part of good workmanship. During the last century most of the arts, save painting

xi

and sculpture of an academic kind, were little considered, and there was a tendency to look on "design" as a mere matter of *appearance*. Such "ornamentation" as there was was usually obtained by following in a mechanical way a drawing provided by an artist who often knew little of the technical processes involved in production. With the critical attention given to the crafts by Ruskin and Morris, it came to be seen that it was impossible to detach design from craft in this way, and that, in the widest sense, true design is an inseparable element of good quality, involving as it does the selection of good and suitable material, contrivance for special purpose, expert workmanship, proper finish and so on, far more than mere ornament, and indeed, that ornamentation itself was rather an exuberance of fine workmanship than a matter of merely abstract lines. Workmanship when separated by too wide a gulf from fresh thought—that is, from design—inevitably decays, and, on the other hand, ornamentation, divorced from workman- ship, is necessarily unreal, and quickly falls into affectation. Proper ornamenta- tion may be defined as a language ad- dressed to the eye; it is pleasant thought expressed in the speech of the tool.

In the third place, we would have this series put artistic craftsmanship before people as furnishing reasonable occupa- tions for those who would gain a liveli- hood. Although within the bounds of academic art, the competition, of its kind, is so acute that only a very few per cent. can fairly hope to succeed as painters and sculptors; yet, as artistic craftsmen, there is every probability that nearly every one who would pass through a sufficient period of apprenticeship to workman- ship and design would reach a measure of success.

In the blending of handwork and thought in such arts as we propose to deal with, happy careers may be found as far removed from the dreary routine of hack labour, as from the terrible uncertainty of academic art. It is desirable in every way that men of good education should be brought back into the productive crafts: there are more than enough of us "in the city," and it is probable that more consideration will be given in this century than in the last to Design and Workmanship.

*   *   *   *   *   *

The designing and making of Costume is a craft—sometimes artistic—with which we are all more or less concerned. It is also, in its own way, one of the living arts, that is, it is still carried forward experimentally by experts directly attached to the "business." It has not yet been subjected to rules of good taste formulated by Academies and Universities; but when Inigo Jones, the great architect, was asked to make some designs for fancy dress, he based them on the Five Orders of Architecture, and ponderous fancies they were.

If we look for the main stem of principle
on which modern Costume develops, we
seem to find it in the desire for freshness,
for the clean, the uncrushed, and the
perfectly fitted and draped. Probably
a modern lady's ideal would be to wear a
dress once, and then burn it.

A correlative of the ideal of freshness
is the delight in perfect "cut," and the
rapidly changing fashions are doubtless
conditioned in part by the desire for the
new and unsullied. "Novelty" is a guar-
antee of newness.

In such ephemeral productions it would
be vain to seek for certain fine types of
excellence which were once common when
dresses were not so lightly cast aside. So
it is necessary that we should understand
what the ruling principle is, for it is one
which will not be set aside at the bidding
of well-meaning reformers. I will only
venture to say that it would be desirable
to make the attempt to separate in some
degree the more constant elements of dress
from those which are more variable. It

will seem a pity to more than outsiders that a " well-dressed " person need wear so little which deserves to have been made by human hands, and nothing which deserves to be preserved. Fine laces and jewels are allowed to be antique—could not the circle of such things be a little broadened? A properly groomed man carries about on him literally nothing worth looking at. We might surely look for a watch-chain with some delicacy of handiwork—something beyond mechanical reductions of iron cables. Fine buttons might conceivably be made to go with the studs, or be made of crystal, amethyst, and silver or gold. Women might allow of the transfer of fine embroidered applications from one dress to another, or make more use of clasps and the like. I am confident that when it is pointed out, it will be felt as a shortcoming that no part of a fine lady's dress need now be too good to throw away. Although the present volume is cast into the form of a history, it is also intended to be a book of suggestions;

and the hope is held that modern dressmakers may refer to it as much as, or
more than, those who are interested in
dress from the historical point of view.

In any case the author's accurate knowledge of the facts, and his many bright
sketches—which are often drawn from
examples in his own remarkable collection
—make the present volume an admirable
handbook of English Costume. The
more technical " patterns " which are in-
cluded amongst the illustrations will be
found most valuable to all who wish to
go deeper than the first glance reveals.

W. R. LETHABY.

1913.

CONTENTS

Contents

	PAGE
GENERAL PREFACE TO THE SERIES	xi
PREFACE	xiv
LIST OF PLATES	xxiii
INTRODUCTION	33

CHAPTER I

Prehistoric Dress—Female	40
Prehistoric Dress—Male	41

CHAPTER II

The Development of Costume to the Tenth Century—Female	45
The Development of Costume to the Tenth Century—Male	49

CHAPTER III

Tenth to the Fifteenth Century—Female	57
Tenth to the Fifteenth Century—Male	71

Contents

CHAPTER IV

PAGE

Fifteenth Century—Female 84

Fifteenth Century—Male 92

CHAPTER V

Sixteenth Century. Character of Trimmings . . 109

Sixteenth Century. Henry VIII—Female . . 113

Sixteenth Century. Henry VIII—Male . . . 118

Sixteenth Century. The Reigns of Edward VI and
Mary—Female 124

Sixteenth Century. The Reigns of Edward VI and
Mary—Male 129

Sixteenth Century. Elizabeth—Female . . . 133

Sixteenth Century. Elizabeth—Male . . . 139

CHAPTER VI

The Character of Trimmings through the Seventeenth
Century 142

    James I 142

    Charles I 143

    The Commonwealth 145

    Charles II 145

    James II and William and Mary . . 146

Seventeenth Century. James I—Female . . . 147

Seventeenth Century. James I—Male . . . 150

Seventeenth Century. Charles I—Female . . . 154

Seventeenth Century. Charles I—Male . . . 160

Seventeenth Century. The Commonwealth—Male and
Female 168

Seventeenth Century. Charles II—Female . . 169

Seventeenth Century. Charles II—Male . . . 174

Seventeenth Century. James II—Female . . . 178

Seventeenth Century. James II—Male . . . 180

Seventeenth Century. William and Mary—Female . 184

Seventeenth Century. William and Mary—Male . 186

CHAPTER VII

The Character of Decoration and Trimmings of the
Eighteenth Century 190

Eighteenth Century. Anne—Female . . . 193

Eighteenth Century. Anne—Male . . . 198

Eighteenth Century. George I—Female . . . 201

Eighteenth Century. George I—Male . . . 207

Eighteenth Century. George II—Female . . 211

Eighteenth Century. George II—Male . . . 214

Eighteenth Century. George III to 1800—Female . 217

Eighteenth Century. George III to 1800—Male . 231

PAGE

Character of Trimmings of the Nineteenth Century . 237

Nineteenth Century. George III—Female . . 241

Nineteenth Century. George III—Male . . . 246

Nineteenth Century. George IV—Female . . 248

Nineteenth Century. George IV, 1820–30—Male . 254

Nineteenth Century. William IV—Female . . 258

Nineteenth Century. William IV—Male . . . 263

Nineteenth Century. Victoria—Female . . . 264

Nineteenth Century. Victoria—Male . . . 273

PATTERNS OF VARIOUS REIGNS FROM ANTIQUE
    COSTUME 276

PATTERNS TO SCALE 283

    „   „   DETAILED LIST . . . 353

INDEX 359

LIST OF DESCRIPTIVE LINES

TO THE

PLATES

FRONTISPIECE . . . . . *Facing Title*

    A Long-trained Muslin Dress, about
    1800.

PLATE I . . . . *Facing p.* 39

    Boots and Shoes from the Fourteenth to
    Nineteenth Century.

PLATE II . . . . . . ,, **42**

    A. Elizabethan Robe in Plush, 1585–
    1605.

    B. Elizabethan Robe in Silk Brocade,
    1565–85.

    C. Elizabethan Male Robe in Velvet
    Brocade, 1580–1615.

    D. Backpiece of Elizabethan Doublet in
    Embroidered Linen, 1580–1605.

xxiii

List of Descriptive Lines to the Plates

PLATE III . . . . *Facing p.* 55

 A. Elizabethan Jump (or Jacket), about 1600.

 B. Portrait of Lady in Embroidered Costume, between 1620 and 1640.

PLATE IV . . . . ,, 58

 C. Youth's Jacket of Linen embroidered in Worsted, 1635–65.

 D. Linen Male Jacket embroidered with Gold and Silk, 1600–40.

PLATE V . . . . ,, 71

 A. Jerkin—Period James I.

 B. Lady's Bodice of Slashed and Van-dyked Satin, 1635–50.

 C. Jerkin of Embroidered Linen, 1630–60.

 D. Jerkin of Embroidered Linen, 1580–1635.

PLATE VI . . . . ,, 74

 A. Collar and Cuffs set with Lace, 1600–30.

 B. Embroidered Leather Jerkin, 1620–1640.

 C. Top of Stocking, Embroidered Linen, 1625–50.

PLATE VII . . . . . . Facing p. 87

    A. Herald's Coat, Embroidered Velvet
        and Silk, First Half Seventeenth
        Century.

    B. Lady's Bodice of Black Velvet,
        1630–60.

    C. Black Silk Jerkin, 1640–50.

PLATE VIII . . . . . . ,, 90

    A. Three Suits—Period Charles II.
    B. ,, ,, ,, ,,
    C. ,, ,, ,, ,,

PLATE VIIIA . . . . . . ,, 103

    A. Suit of Embroidered Silk, 1610–30.

    B. Three Sword-hangers Embroidered
        in Gold, Charles II.

    C. Braided Suit, 1695–90.

PLATE IX . . . . . . ,, 106

    A. Lady's Embroidered Silk Jacket,
        1605–20.

    B. Lady's Bodice of Silk Brocade,
        1680–1700.

PLATE X . . . . . . ,, 119

    A. Black Velvet Bodice, 1600–25.

    B. Five Embroidered Waistcoats, be-
        tween 1690 and 1800.

List of
Descriptive
Lines to the
Plates

XXV

PLATE XI . . . . . . *Facing p.* 122

Sixteen Leather Boots and Shoes, between 1630 and 1850.

PLATE XII . . . . . . „ 135

A. Lady's Outdoor Costume, 1785–95.
B. Costume, Early Eighteenth Century.
C. Silk Brocade Dress, 1760–80.

PLATE XIII . . . . . . „ 138

A. Silk Coat, 1735–55.
B. Brocade Silk Coat, 1745–60.
C. Embroidered Cloth Coat, 1770–90.

PLATE XIV . . . . . . „ 151

A. Embroidered Silk Dress with Pannier, 1765–80.

B. Brocade Dress and Quilted Petticoat, 1750–65.

PLATE XV . . . . . . „ 154

A. White Cloth Coat, 1775–90.
B. Silk Dress, 1740–60.
C. Embroidered Velvet Coat, 1753–75.

PLATE XVI . . . . . . „ 167

A. Silk Brocade Dress, 1740–60.

B. Silk Brocade Sackback Dress, 1755–1775.

C. Dress of Striped Material, 1755–85.

PLATE XVII . . . . . . *Facing p.* 170

    A. Silk Suit, 1765–80.

    B. Quilted Dress, 1700–25.

    C. Silk Embroidered Suit, 1765–80.

PLATE XVIII . . . . . . „ 183

    A. Brocade Bodice, 1770–85.

    B. Flowered Silk Dress, 1750–70.

    C. Silk Brocade Bodice, 1780–95.

PLATE XIX . . . . . . „ 186

    A. Silk Brocade Dress, 1775–85.

    B. Embroidered Silk Jacket, 1775–90.

    C. Brocade Jacket, 1780–95.

PLATE XX . . . . . . „ 199

    A. Gold-embroidered Muslin Dress, 1795–1805.

    B. Nine Aprons, between 1690 and 1750.

    C. Dress of Spotted Stockingette, 1795–1808.

PLATE XXI . . . . . . „ 202

    Twenty-two Boots and Shoes, from 1800 to 1875.

PLATE XXII . . . . . . „ 215

    A. Linen Dress, 1795–1808.

    B. Silk Bodice, 1825–30.

    C. „ „ 1818–25.

List of Descriptive Lines to the Plates

PLATE XXIII . . . . *Facing p.* 218

A. Muslin Dress with Tinsel Design, 1798–1810.

B. Silk Dress, Period George IV.

C. Satin and Gauze Dress, 1820–30.

PLATE XXIV . . . . „ 231

A. Outdoor Silk Jacket, 1798–1808.

B. Embroidered Muslin Bodice, 1816–1830.

C. Embroidered Muslin Bodice, 1824–1825.

D. Satin and Gauze Bodice, 1820–30.

PLATE XXV . . . . „ 234

A. Silk Dress, 1800–10.
B. Cotton Dress, 1800–10.
C. Embroidered Muslin Dress, 1820–30.
D. Silk Gauze Dress, 1824–30.

PLATE XXVI . . . . „ 247

A. Morning Coat of Chintze, 1825–45.
B. Cloth Coat, 1808–20.
C. Cloth Overcoat, 1820–35.

PLATE XXVII . . . . „ 250

Outdoor Silk Dress, 1825–35.

xxviii

PLATE XXVIII . . . . . . *Facing p.* 259

    A. Silk Pelisse, 1820–30.
    B. Cotton Dress, 1830–40.
    C. Silk Spencer and Cape, 1818–27.

PLATE XXIX . . . . . . „ 263

    A. Embroidered Silk Gauze Dress, 1820–30.

    B. Gauze Dress with Appliqued Design, 1825–35.

    C. Printed Linen Outdoor Dress, 1827–1847.

PLATE XXX . . . . . . „ 266

    A. Printed Silk Bodice, 1840–50.
    B. Gathered Linen Bodice, 1837–47.
    C. Silk Bodice and Bertha, 1845–55.

PLATE XXXI . . . . . . „ 270

    A. Embroidered Muslin Outdoor Dress, 1855–65.

    B. Riding Habit, 1845–75.

    C. Gauze Ball Dress, 1840–55.

PLATE XXXII . . . . . . „ 279

    A. Silk Dress, 1860–70.
    B. Gauze Walking Dress, 1850–60.
    C. Silk Dress, 1848–58.

List of
Descriptive
Lines to the
Plates

PLATE XXXIII . . . . . *Facing p.* 282

A. Silk Dress with Court Train, 1828–1838.

B. Silk Afternoon Dress, 1872–78.

C. Silk Coat and Skirt, 1855–56.

XXX

DRESS DESIGN

Plates originally printed
in collotype are now
produced in half - tone

INTRODUCTION

THE subject of Historical Costume covers such a multitude of detail that a volume on each century could be written, with hundreds of illustrations. Thus it is, most works on costume are expensive and bewildering; but I hope this small practical handbook will be a useful addition to the many beautifully illustrated works which already exist.

I have divided the matter into centuries and reigns, as far as possible, in this small work, besides separating male and female attire, thus simplifying reference. A special feature has also been made, of supplying the maker or designer of dress with actual proportions and patterns, gleaned from antique dresses, as far back as they could be obtained; and I am much indebted to the authorities at the Victoria and Albert Museum for the permission given me to examine and measure their unique specimens; also to Mr. Wade, Mr. G. G. ilburne, Mr. Duffield, Mr. Box Kingham, r. Hill, Mr. Breakespeare, and others, for their valuable assistance with interesting specimens. I have used outline drawings in the text, as being more clear for purposes of explanation. The dates given to the illustrations are to be taken as approximate to the time in which the style was worn. Many of the photographs have been arranged from my own costume collection, which has made so much of my research simple, reliable, and pleasant. I am also happy to state that before the final revision of this book I have heard that my collection of historical costumes and accessories will, after a preliminary exhibition at Messrs. Harrod's, be presented to the Victoria and Albert Museum as a gift to the nation by the Directors of that firm. Thus the actual dresses shown in these plates will find a permanent home in London, and become valuable examples to students of costume. The coiffures in the collotype plates are not to be judged as examples, for it would have consumed far too much time to set up these figures more perfectly, but all the bonnets, caps, and accessories given are genuine examples.

In a book of this size, one cannot go into the designs of materials, &c., which is a study any earnest student would not

neglect, but in this connection I would
draw attention to the comparative colour
density and proportion of designs chosen
for various effects.

It has been my endeavour to arrange
a greater variety of the forms which make
up the characters of each period, and also
to give a wider knowledge into the foot-
wear, or details of the footwear, than is
usual in most costume books.

In a review of the styles I would not
press any choice for building new designs,
as I believe in close individual research and
selection, which may utilise many interesting features from costume settings even in
periods which are almost scorned. I believe
the purest beauty is found in the simple
forms of dress and decoration settings from
the 12th to the 15th centuries, schemed to
the natural proportions of the figure. The
grace of line and movement is often aided
by the short train, which can be so happily
caught up in many ways; the slight drag
of the train always keeps the front clear in
outline, besides showing the movement of
the limbs. Length of fall in the material
was desired, the figure creating its own
folds with every turn, but a belt was often
placed rather high under the breast. There

35

is little reason with nature of fine form to
make dress into sections by a corset waist.
A long, lithe, complete curve in outline
—much happier unbroken, except by the
girdle—is certainly the most artistically useful conception, not breaking the rhythm
(as does the harder belt), while it also
induces much beauty in lifting and arranging the drapery. The long falling sleeve
also has the same qualities, giving a greater
fullness of shape, a variety of colour (by a
difference of lining), with a winglike motion,
besides softening the angle of the elbow.

I think the next garment for high esteem
is the chasuble-shaped tunic (with or without sleeves). Falling cleanly from the
shoulders, it stops at a charming length
for the skirt to take up the flow of line.
The delightful effect of partly-laced or
clasped sides was not missed by the ablest
designers. How refined, too, was the
character of decoration of the old period!
The art of concentrating effects is seen
to perfection, retaining the breadth of
shape and length unbroken. Jewelled embroidery of fine enrichment was wrought
on the borders, neck settings, square corners,
the girdle, and the clasps. The precious-
ness of effect was truly appreciated by the

enclosing of the face in the purity of white
lawn and zephyr-like veilings; the circlet
and the long interlaced plaits and charming
nettings were all tastefully schemed. Has
woman ever looked more supreme through
all the centuries of extravagant styles and
distortions? I believe not: but I have
come to the conclusion that, at what-
ever period of seeming insanity of style,
the woman of fine taste can overcome
all obstacles by her individual choice and
"set up," and has really always looked
fascinating.

There was another form of decoration
at this period—the cutting of the edges
into a variety of simple or foliated shapes,
giving a flutter and enrichment to forms
in a simple manner, and this, in conjunction with the increasing richness of materials,
was a valuable aid to lighten the effects.
It was probably initiated by the heraldic
characteristics in vogue.

The pricked and slashed details had much
the same result in enriching surfaces.

Later the fan sleeves of the 18th century
were enhanced in a similar way by the
curved and scalloped shaping, which was
used as late as the Victorian sixties with
happy effect on the polonaises.

37

Now, as regards the finest corset dress, the palm must be given to the sackback dress of the eighteenth century (not in the period of its distortion with hoops), and a full setting showed it to greatest advantage.

This type of design lent itself to more variety in beauty of arrangement than any other; the looping, reefing, and tying always set gracefully in accord with the back fall. The easy exchange of the stomacher also gave additional chance of effect, and the beauty of the fan-shaped sleeve, with its lace falls at the elbow, was a delightful creation. How rich and refined this character could be, without the monstrous forms and head-dresses which later invaded it and turned it into ornate absurdity!

When we examine the period of Charles I, we find much charming dignity in the adaptations of earlier inventions; the collar settings were noble, indeed perfect, in arrangement, and the bodice decoration and proportions most interesting.

For the grace of girlhood no dresses are happier than those of the early 19th century to 1830, and the inventions in trimmings through this period were prolific in beauty and lightness of style.

Analysis of the many fashion-plates and

38

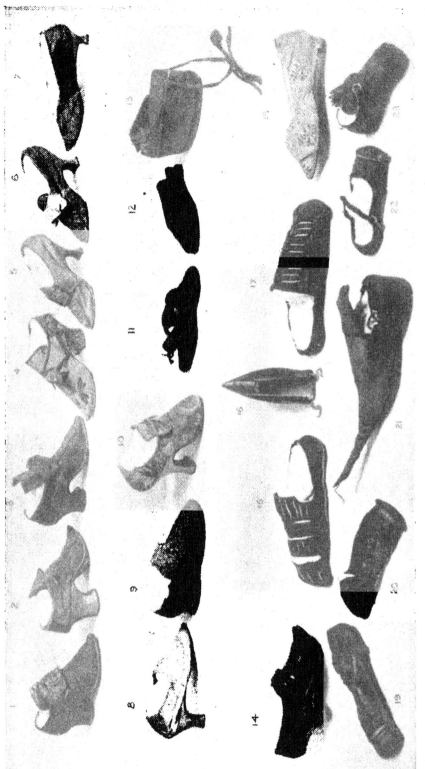

Plate I.—Boots and Shoes from the 14th to the 19th Centuries.

1. Charles II.
2. James II.
3. William and Mary.
4. George II.

6. George III., 1760.
7. George III., 1780-1800.
8. 1870-1880.
9. William and Mary.

11. 1680-1702.
12. 1750-1775.
13. 1580-1625.
14. 1710-1730.

16. Semi-Cloz, 1780-1800.
17. Henry VIII.
18. 1778-1795.
19. Late 15th Century or

20. 1500-1540.
21. Late 14th Century to middle of 15th Century.
22. 1580-1555.
23. 1545-1555.

original dresses of this period will well repay
all interested in beautiful needlecraft and
dress design. The arrangement of frills,
insertions, gathered effects, applied forms,
and tasselled or buttoned additions, will be
found full of beauty and novelty, especially in the dresses of white embroidery.
Plates XXIII and XXIV (see pp. 218–231)
give some happy examples of this time.

A word on the most condemned flow of
fashion during the Victorian era. There
are many dresses of real charm to be found
amongst the mass of heavy styles which
must not be overlooked in studying design
and style. Even the crinoline dress, when
treated with the exquisite silk gauzes, as
Fig. 3 in Plates XXXI and XXXIII (see
pp. 270–282), was as alluring as any woman
could wish, and the original design of the
jacket in the latter figure, with its richly
embroidered, long-skirted front cut short
at the back, arranged itself perfectly on this
type of undersetting. There was notable
refinement of effect and beauty of proportion in many dresses of the sixties, as
exemplified in Fig. A, Plate XXXII (see
p. 279), the waist being set rather high,
and the very full skirt carried back by the
crinoline being held thus with its cross ties.

39

I

CHAPTER I

PREHISTORIC DRESS. FEMALE.

Prehistoric
Dress.
Female

THE woman's attire would have been chiefly a shortish skirt or wrap of coarse linen, wool, or leather, gathered in front or folded at one hip; grass cloth may also have been in use in most primitive tribes. Probably the upper part of the body was kept bare, except for many ornaments and necklaces, but a bodice or jacket cut in the same simple form as the male shirt, with a heavy belt or girdle, would have been used, and certainly a large shawl, which could be wrapped over the head and round the figure during inclement hours. Dyed or painted patterns on the cloths might well have been also in use, their chief designs being stripes, circles or dots, zigzag lines, diamonds and plaid squares, rope patterns and plaited patterns. The hair would have been loose, plaited, or coiled

40

on top, held by bone pins or circlets of
bronze.

PREHISTORIC DRESS. MALE.

We have little description or illustration
to certify the actual dress of the early
inhabitants of Britain, but we can draw
conclusions with pretty certain assurance,
from the knowledge of their mode of living.
From their attainments in artistic design
and handiwork, it is clear they had arrived
at a very high state of savage culture
before the Roman invasion; and we have
only to study the better types of savage
life still in progress, to picture how our
own primitive race would be likely to dress
under the conditions of climate. The
thousands of "finds," which accumulate
evidence every year, give us a closer ac-
quaintance with their customs and work.
The rest we must imagine from our
general knowledge of what they had to
contend with in climate, forest, cave, and
floods.

These early people, it is presumed from
certain discoveries, had long known the
art of coarsely weaving flax and wool,
which must soon have been in general use,

41

from its being healthier and cleaner than the garments of skin. And very probably a coarse linen, with simple dyes of red, blue, yellow, and brown, was in use here when the Romans came.

The head-dress consisted of a cap of fur or wool, probably decorated with a feather, over loose and most likely very unkempt hair falling to the shoulders. The Gauls cut their locks from the back of the head, often tying up the remainder in a tuft on the top; no doubt the hair was sometimes plaited or pinned up with wood, bone, or bronze ornaments. Bone pins, teeth, and boar tusks were carried in the ears, as well as studs of bone or stone in the underlip, and even the cheek may have been so decorated, as it was amongst the Esquimaux. The face and body were painted with red and white ochre and a blue stain. The neck was adorned with strings of teeth, stones, amber, jet, bronze, and probably beads of glass or baked clay coloured. Amulets and tokens, armlets and bracelets were all in use. Also the torque, a twisted rod of gold flattened or curled together at the ends, was a mark of dignity. A wristlet of wood, bone, or leather was worn when the bow and arrows were used.

42

Plate II.—(*a*) Elizabethan Robe in Plush. 1585-1605.
(*b*) Elizabethan Robe in Silk Brocade. 1565-85.
(*c*) Elizabethan Male Robe in Velvet Brocade. 1580-1615.
(*d*) Back-piece of Elizabethan Doublet in Embroidered Linen. 1580-1605.

Measures, see p. 281.   *Sleeve pattern of C, see p. 300.*

Facing page 42.

The arms were a spear of flint or bronze and a dagger of the same, a hatchet or heavy club, a mace studded with flint or bronze spikes, and the sling, which would have necessitated a leather wallet to carry the stones; fish spears and snags. Also the bolas for felling cattle seems to have been known; in fact nearly all the usual implements appertaining to savage life were in use.

The first item of male attire was of two skins fastened at the shoulders, and from this we get the early chasuble form (which may be so beautifully treated, even to the present time), girt with a leather thong or strap at the waist. One skin lapped the other, and hardly needed sewing together at the sides, while thus it was easier to throw off; it may also have been tied up between the legs. The fur was worn both inside and out, according to the weather; this large skin wrap would also be worn crossways with the right shoulder free, and the simple cloak of various lengths with a hole for the head to pass through was no doubt one of the first discoveries in costume.

A loin cloth or skin may have been worn alone, caught up through the legs and fastened at the back of the waist with

43

a heavy belt and set well down the hips.
This would hold a number of personal
necessities, in the shape of a wallet and
dagger. The legs would be wrapped with
skins, tied up or crossed by leather or
sinew thongs, or with hemp or grass
rope. Skins were probably also used on
the feet, gathered and tied above the
instep and round the ankle.

The enumeration of these items will
give a pretty definite idea of how the early
race would appear in their more or less
attired form. In fighting, they cleared for
action (as it were) and discarded all cloth-
ing, their only protection being a shield of
wicker or wood covered with leather; it
may have been studded with bronze plates
or painted with grotesque characters, as
were their own bodies, in true savage style,
to strike fear into their enemies; it is even
possible feather decorations formed part of
their " get up."

CHAPTER II

THE DEVELOPMENT OF COSTUME TO THE TENTH CENTURY. FEMALE.

THE female head-dress consisted chiefly of flowing hair banded with a circlet of various shapes, but a development of braid-ing plaits is found very early, and the hair was probably arranged so before the Roman era. These plaits were generally brought over the shoulder to the front, the hair being parted in the centre, thus making an oval forehead. Various caps began to show originality, and jewels were set in the centre of the forehead on the little crown-like hat, which must have been most becoming. Squares of coloured stuffs were draped over the head and shoulders, some-times upon white linen squares, and many ladies began to bind the face and head, shutting out the hair, in the 8th century. The kerchief draping is very important to

45

study, because it was the general mode amongst the people.

Heavy collars of ornament and strings of beads, hanging even to the waist, are noticeable features of these centuries, also large ear-rings.

A full cloak, with a large clasp or brooch, opened in front, or was turned to free one shoulder; there was also a long "drape" thrown round over the opposite shoulder or brought picturesquely over the head.

The ecclesiastical form of cloak as described in the male attire was also formed about the 6th century; its graceful line was frequently bordered completely with a band of ornament, and it was clasped just across the breasts.

The complete circular cloak, with a hole for the head, is seen very early, decorated with a pinked edge, which may also be noted on some of the short dresses of the middle classes. Aprons are no doubt of the earliest origin. A loose tunic falling to the hips was girded rather high up the body, as in the classic dress, and bands passing both outside or crossing between the breasts and going over the shoulder came from the same source; these were with, or without, short sleeves to the elbow. A long

46

Saxon Type

Stephen

FIG. 1.

loose robe was the chief attire to the 6th century, belted rather high in the waist, and caught up with a girdle at the hips; these girdles gave a great interest to the early centuries, with the art of arranging the fullness of skirt into its hold.

From the 6th century the dress became closer fitting, and a short bodice is seen; the neck was cut very low, either square or round in shape, and this style had short tight sleeves or tight sleeves to the wrist. The later tunic of the 9th century marked the beginning of the slit-open upper sleeve, and a greater length of the neck opening, which came to be fastened down the front to the waist.

The early skirts (to the 6th century) were hung from the hips, and were often attached to a heavy girdle band, the fullness was gathered mostly at the back and front; other skirts hung from a higher belt and were again caught up in the girdle. A V-shaped neck setting was worn by the Franks, from which probably came the shaped front piece that will interest us in the 13th century. The shoes were similar to the male shapes described later, and the same mode of binding the stockings was sometimes imitated.

48

THE DEVELOPMENT OF COSTUME TO
THE TENTH CENTURY. MALE.

The Devel-
opment of
Costume to
the Tenth
Century.
Male

In taking the long period from the
Roman occupation to the 10th century,
we can discover a real development of
style in costume, as with the system of
vassalage a distinction of class arose. No
doubt the Romans introduced a finer
tuition of weaving, needlecraft, decoration,
and dyeing; and later the various peoples
coming from the Continent, when settled
under Alfred in the 9th century, produced
a solid style of barbaric splendour.

The male hair dressing, from the rugged
mass of hair, soon became well combed
and trimmed square across the neck: ear-
rings may still have been in use by some
nobles till the 11th century, and chaplets
were worn upon the hair. The Saxon
beard was divided into two points. Small
round tight caps of wool, fur, or velvet,
and rush or straw hats of a definite shape
were in use to the 10th century. Tight
caps, with lappets tied under the chin, and
hoods appear on the short capes about the
8th century, or probably earlier. The
garment was of the simplest form, cut

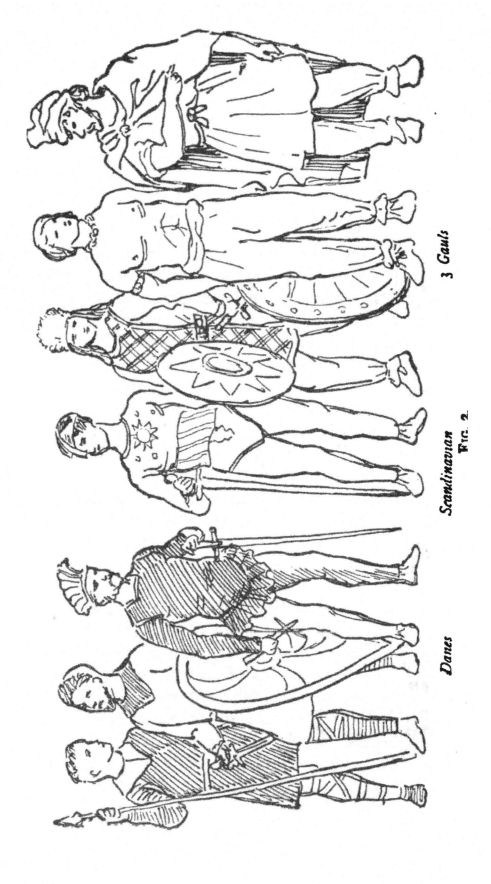

Danes

Scandinavian

3 Gauls

Fig. 2.

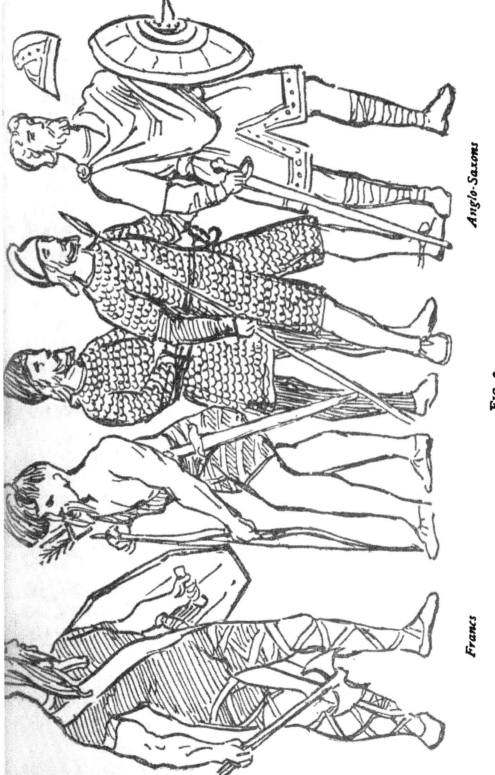

Anglo-Saxons

Franks

FIG. 3.

The Devel-
opment of
Costume to
the Tenth
Century.
Male

like a plain square loose shirt to the middle of the thigh, and this was put on over the head. The opening to pass the head through was the first part to receive a band of decoration. The sides were sometimes opened to the hips and the front caught between the legs and held at the waist. A garment opened down the front, and another wrapped across to either shoulder is also seen. A belt girt the waist, and the tunic was pulled loosely over it. This also carried the essential requirements in the shape of a pouch, dagger, knife, comb, sword, &c. The neck was ornamented with chains of bronze, gold, beads, and charms, and up to the 8th century a bronze ornamental armlet was worn, besides a wristlet.

The men of the ruling class from the 8th century were clothed in a long garment of simple shape, falling to the ankle, richly bordered at the hem and neck. This generally had long tight sleeves, and often over this a shorter tunic, reaching just below the knee, sometimes sleeveless, or with rather full sleeves tightening to the wrist.

A plain square chasuble shape was in fashion from the 8th century, reaching to

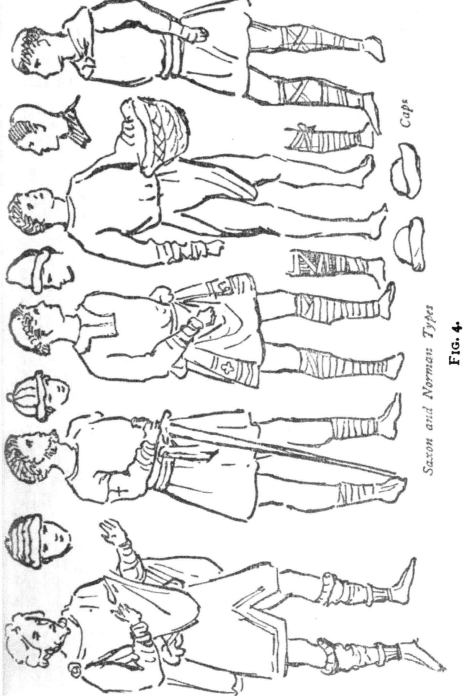

Caps

Saxon and Norman Types   FIG. 4.

The Devel-
opment of
Costume to
the Tenth
Century.
Male

the bottom of the calf of the leg, and richer materials began to be used; no belt was passed round this, as it was allowed to fall straight.

Loose breeches were worn from very early times, and a loose trouser to the ankle, being tied there or bound crosswise from the boot sometimes right up the thigh. The same binding was done even with the bare legs and later hose: close-fitting short breeches and cloth hose became a feature in the 10th century, and with the latter an ornamental knee-piece or garter below the knee sometimes finished the strappings.

The cloak was the "grand garment," heavily banded with ornament and fastened with a large clasp on one shoulder, or at the centre of the breast. Long circular cloaks of varying lengths, put on over the head, were much favoured, and when caught up at the sides on either shoulder gave a fine draped effect.

Another cloak of ecclesiastical character, sloping in a curve from the neck and not meeting in front, is seen on many notable figures from the early 8th century, large clasps bridging the width low down on the chest.

Plate III.   (a) Elizabethan Jump (or Jacket).   About 1600.   (b) Portrait of a Lady in Embroidered Costume.   Between 1620 and 1640.

No doubt the sandal of various forms was much used for footwear through this period, also a simple low shoe which was held on by the leg-strappings, as, about the 8th century, shoes are seen with loops at the upper edge, these being attachments

FIG. 5.—TYPES OF SHOES.
British, Roman, Norman to 13th century.

for the binding, and this was no doubt a method from the prehistoric times.

There was also a soft boot reaching to the calf, laced up the front; and, after the 8th century, a rather pointed shoe, open down the instep, laced, tied, or gathered into a buckle about the ankle.

CHAPTER III

TENTH TO THE FIFTEENTH CENTURY.
FEMALE.

THE head-dress of women now began to show a preference to confine the hair with nets and to close in the face, which continued till the 15th century. The circlet and long plait or plaits and the flowing hair remained till the 14th century. In the 12th century we discover the hair gathered in nets at either side of the head, covering the ears. A low-crowned hat was bound over with a band of lawn or fine material passing underneath the chin, otherwise the plaits were looped up under a circlet which was also worn with the flowing hair.

A square effect was aimed at in the 13th century with tight side-plaits bound into a shape or netted hair was strapped to the head as in Fig. 11 (see p. 65). A fall of

57

fine material softened the hard effect, and many ladies of quality bound the face, neck, and head in the wimple of fine linen, sometimes gathering this to the same quaint shape of the netted hair. I give a variety of these settings on page 65. A kerchief of linen coming round the neck was brought up tightly round the face and festooned on the top of the head, while another piece was pinned close to the brows and fell loosely to the shoulders, being often held on by a circlet as well.

This character was maintained till the early 14th century, when a style of high peaked hats came into evidence, one shape of which became the most imposing feature of historic costume in the 15th century. It was still but a simple form in the middle of the 14th century, for another shape first gained predominance. Early in this century also may be noted a curious shape like the cap of liberty, usually with a long tail at the back as drawn on page 59. This carried design to the eccentric forms of the pig-tailed hood, and then the rival of the high peaked hat took its place towards the end of the 14th century—a cushioned head-dress, which rose and divided in a hornlike structure. It

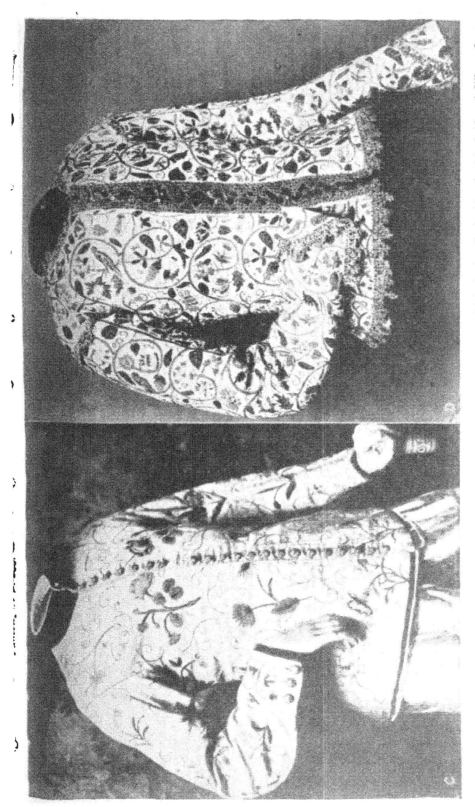

Plate IV.—(c) Youth's Jacket of Linen Embroidered in Worsted. 1635-65. (d) Linen Male Jacket Embroidered with Gold and Silk. 1600-40.

Fig. 6.—Tenth to thirteenth century.

Henry II.

John

Henry I.

Richard I.

FIG. 7.

Fig. 8.—Twelfth to fourteenth century.

started as in Fig. 25, and I have illustrated its progress; the veil draping was a great feature, giving plenty of scope for individual fancy. It was, as a rule, richly decorated with gold and jewels, and the hair was completely enclosed in a gold net and a tight-fitting cap to hold this erection. Large drop ear-rings were much worn, and a fine chain of gems encircled the neck or fell to the breast.

In the 10th century a long close-fitting robe was in fashion, sometimes with a deep V-shaped neck opening, though usually the neck was cut to a round form. Some sleeves were tighter with a small cuff, but usually the outer garment had a falling sleeve with a square or round end showing the tight under-sleeve. The outer sleeve varied much in length, from the elbow or hand dropping even to the ground; it was narrow and widened through the 14th century, when its edge was cut into various patterns as in Fig. 18 (see p. 79). In the 13th century we notice a long sleeve opened at the elbow for the under sleeve to come through, which beautiful style continued to the middle of the 17th century.

With the 10th century came the first corselet from the waist to the hip, clasp-

62

Norman, 12th century

Saxon, 12th century

FIG. 9.

FIG. 10.—Fourteenth century, 1st half.

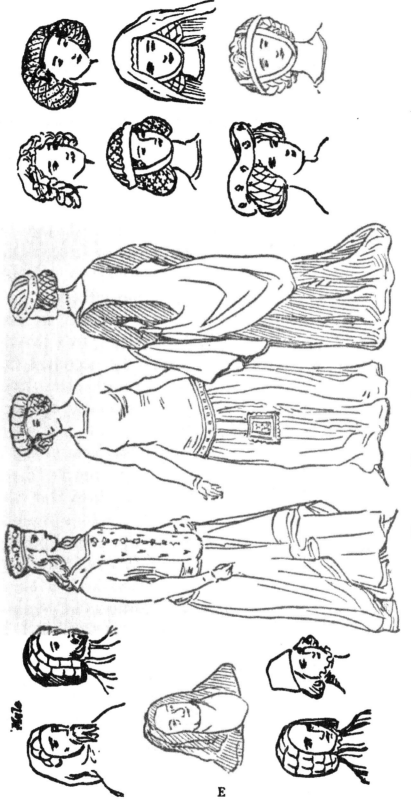

Fig. 11.—Fourteenth century, 2nd half

ing a loose tunic with an under-dress taking a long pointed train. The manner of tucking the tunic under the corselet when it was worn over it, and so creating festoons, is worthy of notice as interesting in arrangement and design.

The 13th century parti-coloured and striped dresses foreshadowed the heraldic fashion, which must be studied for its proportion and treatment of decorative colour-values in counterchange to get the true value of its noble effects.

A great feature now appears in the chasuble-shaped front or setting to a closely cut jacket. This ultimately becomes the decorative stomacher through the later periods, and it is very interesting to note its development.

In the 13th century this jacket was a fur construction of a long simple form opened at the sides to the hips for the sleeves to come through; it had a straight hem or was rounded at the front points, and a chasuble form of it was treated as in Fig. 13 or in conjunction with a short cape; it was chiefly a decoration of ermine. It grew into a complete jacket, and in the 14th century it was heavily ornamented with gems; and the simple front, from

66

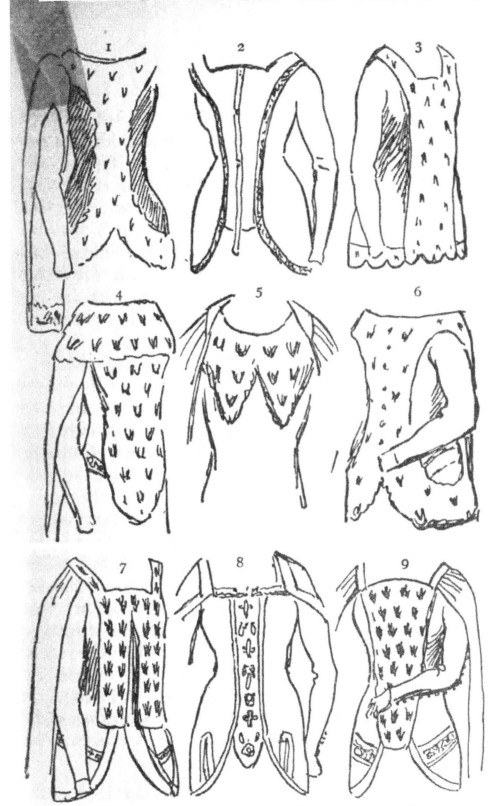

FIG. 12.—Nos. 1 to 7, 14th century. Nos. 8 and 9, 15th century.

being a feature outside the jacket, was later often enclosed at the sides. The jacket itself is beautiful in form and proportion, and the curved band of design over the hips makes a nice foil to the curved front. This pattern is plainly derived from the effect of the rich girdle that was at first seen through the side openings and few jackets are without it, the usual shaping of the neck with most of these was square.

In the first quarter of the 14th century the setting of the neck was of a round shape, and after 1350 a raised or curved form is favoured. Later still, and with the hornlike head-dress, a very deep V shape, open almost to the belt was the mode, often being filled in with velvet. At the same time some began to take up the fashions of a very high collar and a round-shaped body and sleeves, as in Fig. 24 (see p. 89), with which a wide pointed belt is seen. Some robes were opened in front up to the height of the girdle, though many dresses were worn without girdles after the 12th century. Decorated pockets are sometimes seen in the later period, and an interesting hand-covering or falling cuff came with them.

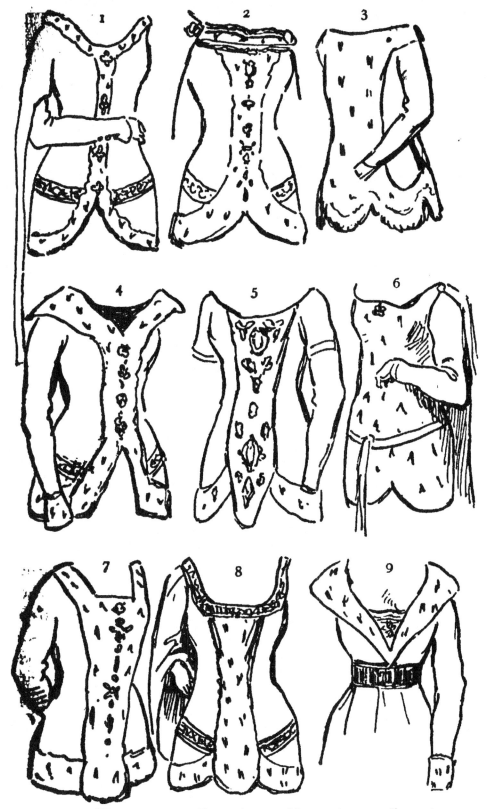

FIG. 13.—Nos. 1 to 3, 14th century.   Nos. 4 to 9, 15th century.

The cloak as described in the 10th century still continued till the 12th, as well as the light wrap which may almost be placed with any period, though mostly a feature of the more classic styles.

Skirts and underskirts were worn with trains. They were mostly banded with wide borders of ornament up to the 13th century, the fullness being often gathered to the back and front.

The chasuble-shaped overdress was worn to the middle of the 14th century, sleeveless, and, laced or sewn tight to the figure from the arm to the hip, or completely down the sides, generally reached just below the knee.

The shoes were of much the same character as those of the male examples illustrated, though they hardly reached the same extravagance in length, owing, no doubt, to the feet of woman being hampered by her skirt; but I suspect they even braved high wooden clogs, as we know they did the tall chopins of the 16th century, to heighten their stature.

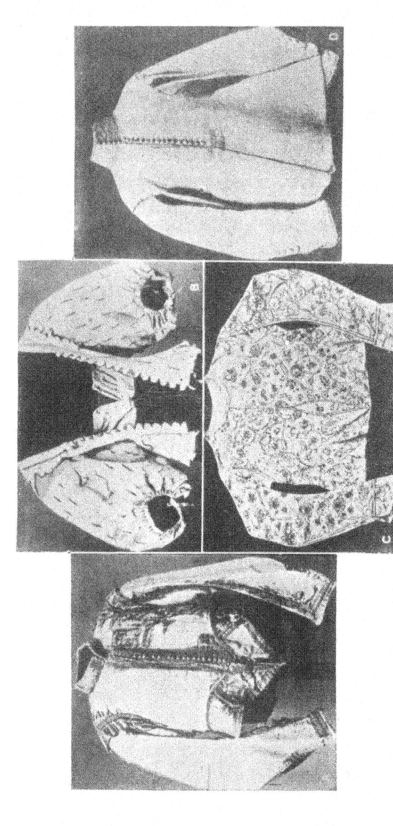

Pattern measurements, see p. 293.

Plate V.—(**a**) Jerkin. Period James I. (**b**) Lady's Bodice ot Slashed and Vandyked Satin. 1635-50. (**c**) Jerkin of Embroidered Linen. 1630-60. (**d**) Jerkin of Embroidered Linen. 1580-1635.

TENTH TO THE FIFTEENTH CENTURY.
MALE.

From the 10th to the 15th century, we find costume developing rapidly into elaborate and interesting designs. Close relations with the Continent brought new ideas, and rich velvets and brocades interwoven with gold enhanced the gorgeousness of attire, while the introduction of heraldic design brought in a very picturesque element. Hats and head-dresses began to become important features, enlarging to eccentric shapes and proportions, only equalled in the extravagant part of the 18th century.

It may be noted that feminine fashion, as it assumes new characters and proportions, affects the style of the male clothes in the same way, as, when a high or pointed head-dress comes in, the male hat also increases its size; the same with curved or angular designs, full or tight sleeves.

The hair was worn long and rather squared in shape at the back till the end of the 15th century. A tendency to shut in the face by close hoods tied under the chin is remarked, and this forms a strong feature of the 13th and 14th centuries. Ear-rings were seldom worn after the 10th century; but the neck was generally adorned with heavy chain decorations.

Beards assumed a pointed shape in accordance with this development of fashion, and double-pointed beards were revived between 1380 and 1386. Hats of straw with mushroom brims and round tops came into vogue in the 11th century, covered with coloured materials and finished with a spike or button at the top, and the crowns of these took a pointed shape in the 14th century. The usual cap with folded brim had a loose crown, and we find this began to lengthen and fall over to one side in the 11th century, and continued to elongate till, in the 15th century, it often dropped to the knee in a long thin point. In the 14th century it took a fullness of loose folds, with serrated or foliated edges falling to the shoulder as in Fig. 15 (see p. 73). A close helmet-shaped cap is seen in the 12th century, with a falling point from the crown, and the 13th century brought in the higher crowned hat, with a long peaked front, turned up at the back. Feathers were worn at the front, back, or side of hats, and sometimes on the

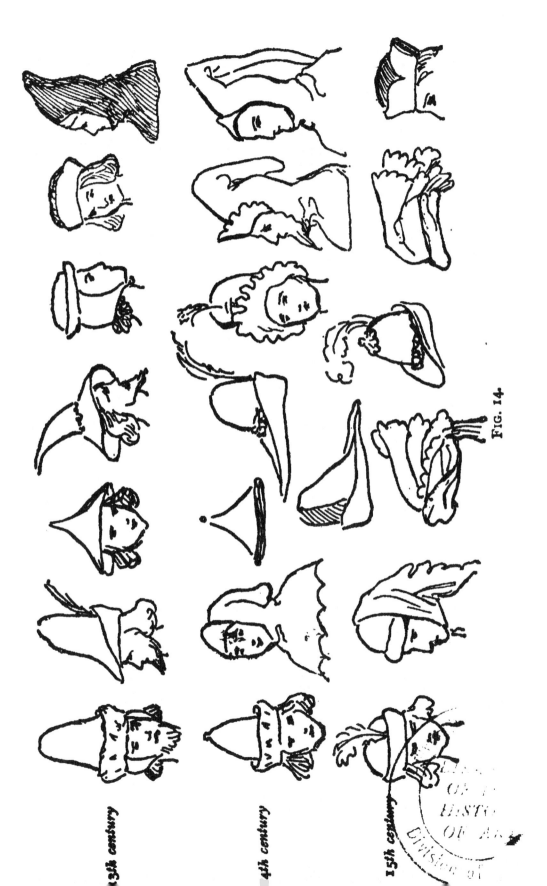

FIG. 14.

13th century

14th century

15th century

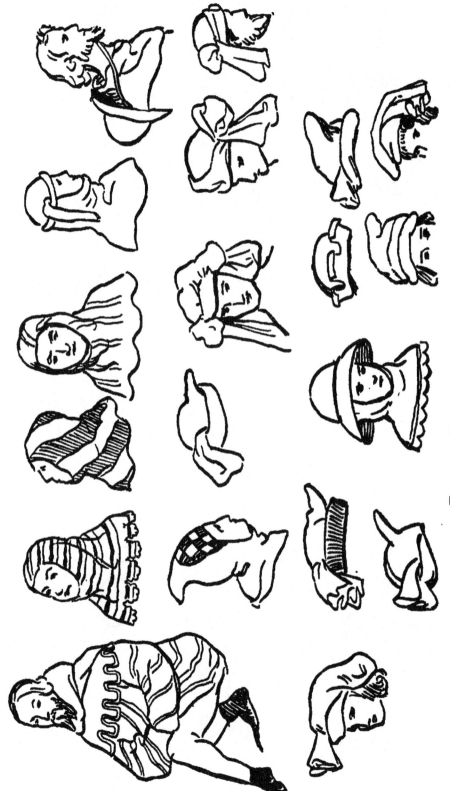

Fig. 15.—Fourteenth century.

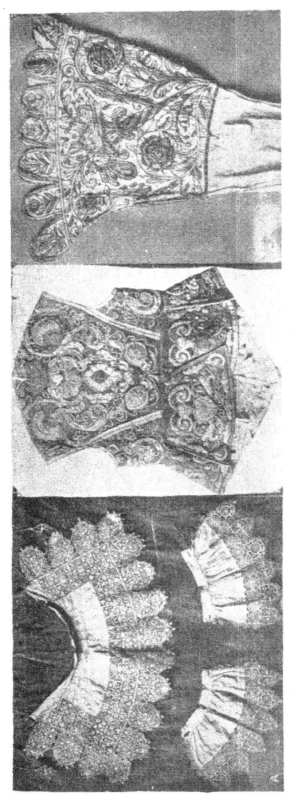

Plate VI.—(*a*) Collar and Cuffs set with Lace. 1600–30. (*b*) Embroidered Leather Jerkin. 1620–40. (*c*) Top of Stocking. Embroidered Linen. 1625–50.

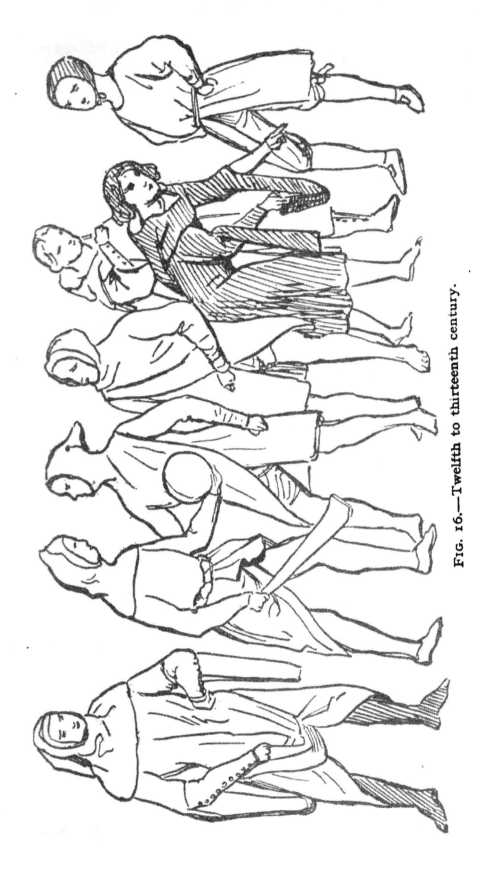

FIG. 16.—Twelfth to thirteenth century.

front of the hoods; these increased their dimensions in height and peak, till the straight-up high hat, which was often brimless, came in the 15th century. The early hood or cowl soon began to vary its design, for in the 13th century it was often a part of, or attached to, a chasuble shape falling back and front, or with the long front, stopping at a short cape length behind. A note of interest in the 14th century appears, where the forehead part of the hood is turned up, showing a coloured lining, and at times the fashionable serrated edge surrounding the face is seen.

The chasuble-shaped garment was a feature often worn over the coat until the end of the 15th century, and was generally worn long with the elongated fashion of the 14th century, and short with the shorter tunics of the 15th century. They are found very wide in the 14th century, and so fall well down over the shoulder, where they are often laced a short distance up, creating an interesting feature. Cloaks were not so much in favour with the heavier cowl and cape, but they were used, fastened by brooches to either shoulder rather at the back, after the 12th century.

A very tight-fitting suit called Justacorps

FIG. 17.—Fourteenth century.

came into use from the 12th century, and
developed a padded round-shaped body
towards the end of the 14th century; the
closely-cut body was buttoned up to the
throat, or was set with a high collar for the
first time. The tights came over it, sometimes rather high up the waist, being laced
to it. A long tunic was chiefly favoured
during the 10th and 11th centuries with
short or long cuffless sleeves, and a full
bell-shaped falling sleeve showed a close-
fitting under one.

These tunics were chiefly open at the
neck as in the earlier times, though a slight
difference to be noted is a V-shaped opening in the 14th century, which is developed
in the 15th century; they were also split
up the sides, even to the hips. Some were
very full in shape, and were gathered to
either side as in the illustration; others
had the body closely fitted and full only in
the skirt, but as a rule one finds this latter
shape only reaches just below the knee.
They were often tucked into the belt in
front, showing a rich under-skirt.

A girdle (besides a belt) was worn on
the hips with the longer tunics, as in Fig.
28 (see p. 94), the dagger and pouch
being carried in front on the girdle, and

78

FIG. 18.—Fourteenth century.

not the belt. A small dagger was often slung at the back or front of the neck as an ornament at the end of the 14th century.

Tights to the waist were worn with both long and short tunics, and retained the crossed binding up the legs to the 13th century, in the various designs of page 53. Parti-coloured tights came in with the 14th century, carrying out the heraldic character of dress, and this may be found till about 1530. A sandal shoe was much worn up to the 12th century, with strappings to various heights up the leg, this even over the short top-boots, but the usual shoe opened down the front of the instep to the toe, which was rather pointed in shape, and it was curved or square at the ankle. The illustration gives a good variety of the prevalent forms. The stocking-boot is also another characteristic of this earlier time, as well as the commoners' woollen gaiters, worn as in Fig. 30, on the seated figure, which were in use to the middle of the 16th century.

In the illustrations which show no shoe on the tights, it will be understood that a sole of leather was sewn on to the under part of the foot. This practice is even seen

FIG. 19.—Twelfth and thirteenth centuries.

F

to-day on the Continent, where the clog is
mostly in use. A soft boot, reaching to
the calf, was worn till the 15th century,
with the top folded or trimmed with fur,
the latter being generally laced down the
front, even to the instep: the shape of
these only varied in the length of the
pointed toes as the style developed.

The long-pointed shoes began to increase
all through the 13th century, and in the
14th century they reached their greatest
length, when the points were often tied up
to a garter just below the knee. Wooden
clogs were much used, and were often considerably raised. Iron circular supports
were also in use at the end of this time;
these were the foretaste of the eccentric
chopins of the 16th century, which were
more favoured on the Continent than here.
The pointed toes also were made to curl
outwards, giving a splay-footed effect, late
in the 14th century.

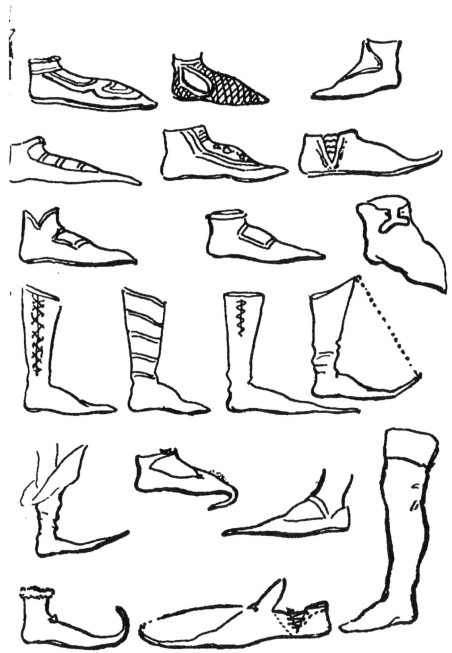

FIG. 20.—Fourteenth and fifteenth centuries.

CHAPTER IV

FIFTEENTH CENTURY. FEMALE.

Fifteenth Century. Female

WE have now arrived at the height of eccentric fashion in mediæval head-dress. The hornlike creations, studded with jewels, and peaks of wondrous height, both draped with fine muslins and often completely shutting away the hair from sight, had a supporting cap which mostly came over ears and cheeks, and a clutch is seen on the forehead, at times concealed by a jewel. The hair was generally allowed to fall loose under the back drape, or a long plait is sometimes seen at the back with the first-named head-dress. The back drape setting from the brow down the back was well conceived to balance the high spire, but it seems to have been discarded during the reign of Edward V, and light veil falls were worn which often came half over the face. In Henry VII's time the extreme

84

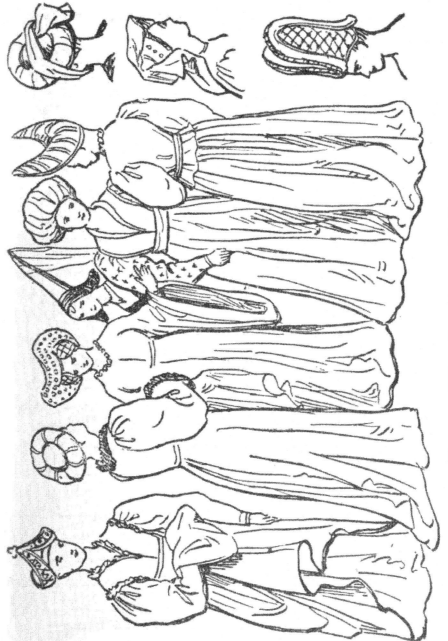

FIG. 21.—Fifteenth century, 1st half.

FIG. 22.—Middle of fifteenth century to sixteenth century.

Measurement, see p. 297.

Plate VII.—(**a**) Herald's Coat. Embroidered Velvet and Silk. 1st half
17th Century. Measured pattern, page 301.
(**b**) Lady's Bodice of Black Velvet. 1630–60.
(**c**) Black Silk Jerkin. 1640–60.

Facing page 87.

FIG. 23.—Fifteenth century, 1st half.

fashion came in the shape of a closely-fitting curved cap, with a fall of material over the back. The ermine-trimmed jacket was still in favour to the middle of the last-named reign, when it was worn low down over the hips.

The chief dress of this period had a V-shaped collar-front meeting at the waist, mostly made in black material or fur. It was wide on the shoulder, and seems to have been stiffened to set out; the V shape was generally filled in with velvet, and a very wide band encircled the waist; a girdle is occasionally noted. The keys' pocket and other requisites were generally carried on the underskirt during these times. The skirt was full and gathered to the back in a train, the gathers often running into the bodice; a very wide border is prevalent, even to the middle of the thigh. Tight sleeves are usual, and hanging sleeves were worn, mostly set in a very short sleeve, which assume a puff-shape in Henry VII's reign; long cuffs, almost covering the hand, are seen on many sleeves.

Modes of opening the skirt up to the hips occasionally showed themselves, and even the sides to the hips are seen laced. In the earlier dress, about 1485, the neck

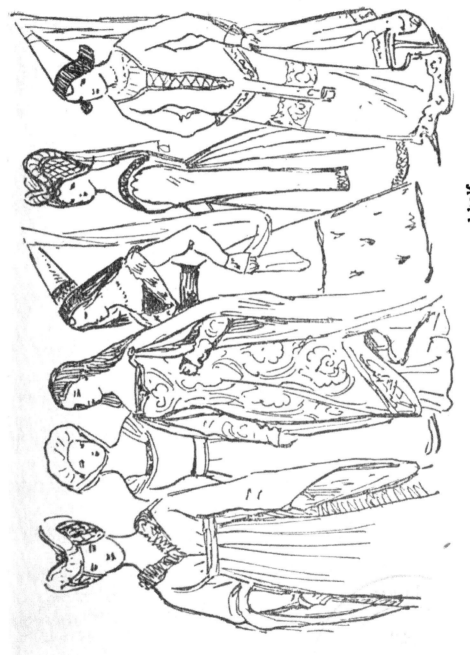

FIG. 24.—Fifteenth century, 2nd half.

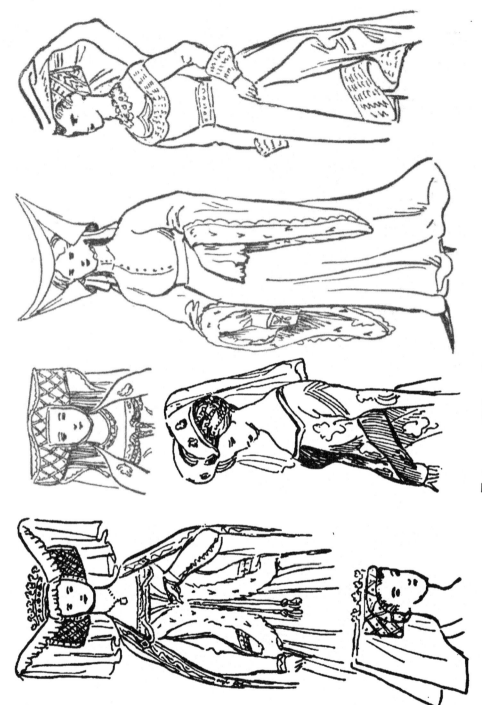

FIG. 25.—Fifteenth century, 2nd half

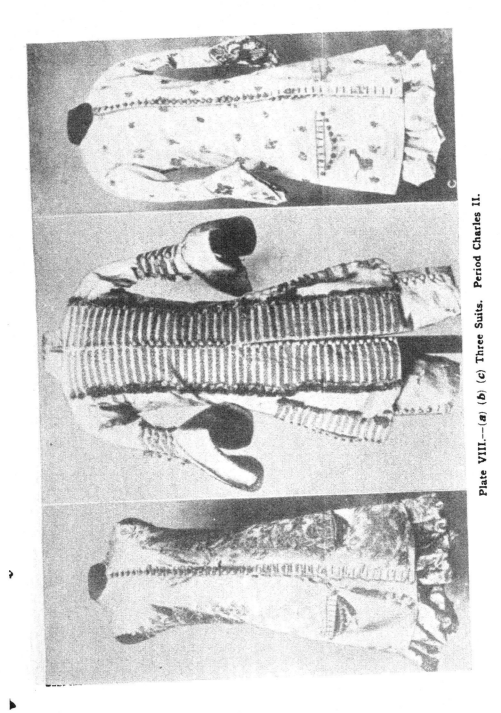

Plate VIII.—(*a*) (*b*) (*c*) Three Suits. Period Charles II.

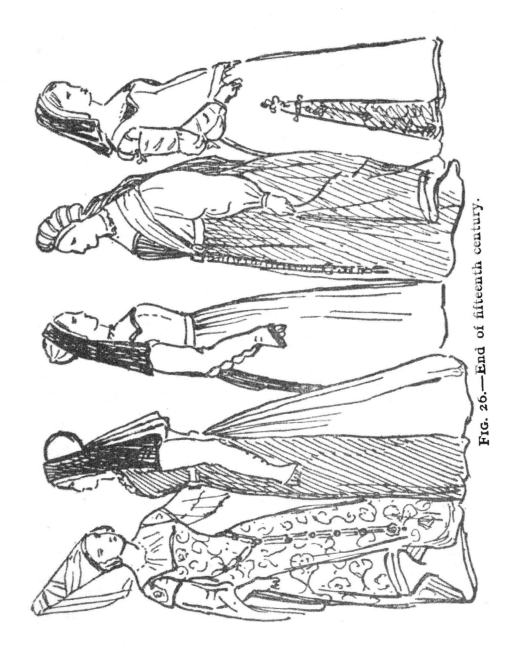

Fig. 26.—End of fifteenth century.

setting of dress became very square, and was filled with fine-drawn lawn. The square shape rises in a curved centre before the end of this period, and a close-fitting robe was worn with a girdle, often opened up the sides. The short upper sleeve and full outer sleeve so much in vogue gave place to a divided upper and lower sleeve, laced or tied with ribbon, with puffs of lawn pulled through the openings at shoulder and elbow, and down the back of the fore-arm. Slashes are now seen in most sleeves, and an Italianesque character pervaded the fashion.

High, soft boots and shoes of a similar shape to the male description were worn, and changed when the square-toe shoes came in.

Through this period there are many interesting details of costume to study, while gilt tags, finishing laces, and ribbons are to be remarked from this period.

FIFTEENTH CENTURY. MALE.

The chief shapes to mark in this century in male head-dress is the increased height of the tall hats which rise to vie with the female fashions. We still see a round hat

FIG. 27.—Fifteenth century.

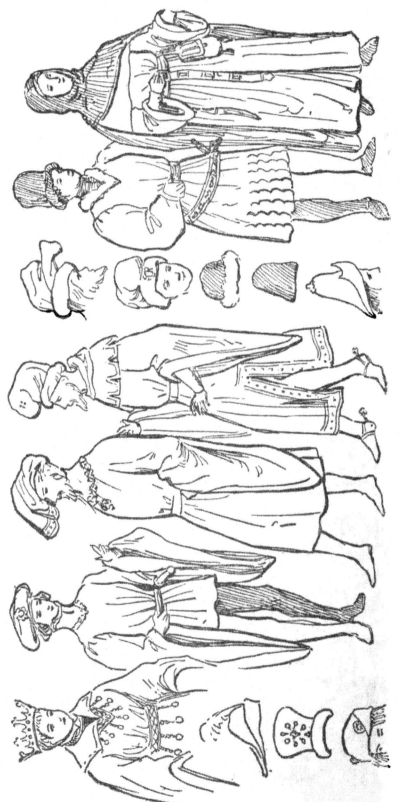

Fig. 28.—Fifteenth century, 1st half.

FIG. 29.—Middle of fifteenth century.

with a rolled edge and long fall over one side, besides shorter folds in the crown, both scalloped or foliated at the edge, and this shape may be noted till about 1460. Some of these hats were made without a crown, as in Fig. 28 (see p. 94); the roll was decorated, as a rule, with jewelled studs. A top hat, something like our present shape, appears, but more belled at the top and also a padded, rolled brim. It was made in various rich materials, and often decorated with jewels. The peak-fronted hat still continued to be favoured till about 1480, its chief difference being a crown more eccentric in height. Tall cylinder hats, with folded brims or no brim, and other shapes are illustrated. The variety is so great through this period that it is well to study the vagaries of fashion which I have illustrated in sequence as far as possible; they were mostly used till about the last quarter of this century, when the low-crowned flat hat with turned-up brim began to secure the fashion. This was generally worn tilted on one side and often over a scarlet skull-cap. A large bunch of plumes came in with this hat, set up from the front, curving backwards, and giving a very grand effect: with most

FIG. 30.—Fifteenth century.

G

FIG. 31.—Fifteenth century, 1st half.

FIG. 32.—Fifteenth century, 2nd half.

of the tall hats the feather was set at
the back.

The notable change in the tunic, which
was worn both very short and to the
ground, was the arrangement of folds to
the back and front, gathered to a V shape
at the waist. The hanging sleeve began
to go out of favour after the middle of
the century, but the sleeve or cuff covering the hand was continued till the end of
this century.

A sleeve, full at the shoulder, is found,
and short, round, padded sleeves came
in, worn over a close-fitting sleeve.
This short sleeve became raised on the
shoulder, and was cut or looped up the
outer side: a long loose outer sleeve is
also seen in conjunction with these short
ones. A very short jacket is notable, of
a plain square shape, with a plain sleeve on
the left arm and a hanging sleeve on the
right to the knee. The tight-fitting jerkin,
laced down the front, was worn with this
as with most other coats.

The high collar to the throat had gone
out for a collar opened in front. Very
short and very long "chasubles" were
worn with or without sleeves which were
gathered high and full at the shoulders.

100

Fig. 33.—End of fifteenth century.

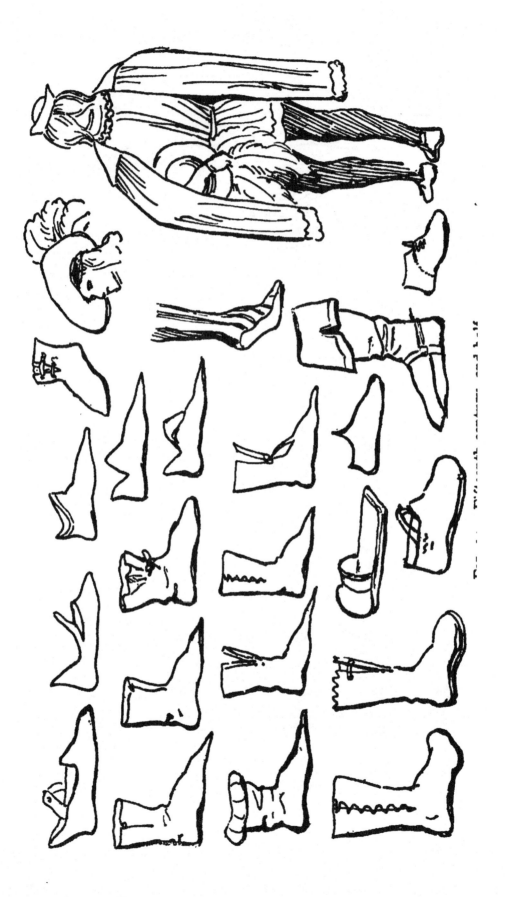

Fig. 44. Fifteenth costume and belt

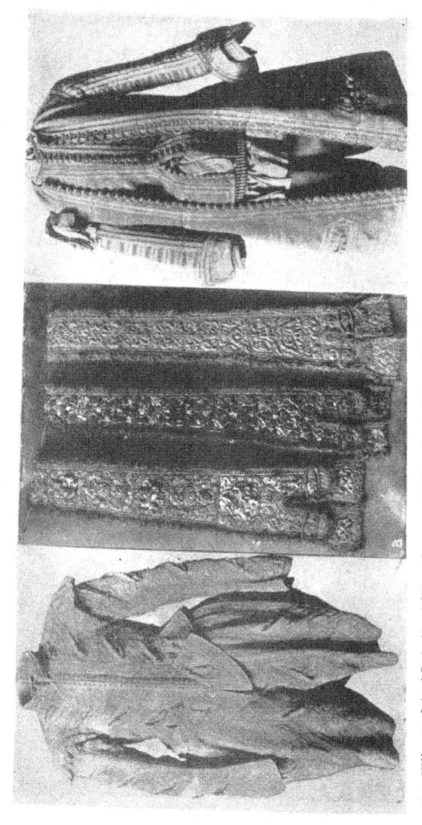

Plate VIIIa—(*a*) Suit of Embroidered Silk. 1610–30. (*b*) Three Sword Hangers Embroidered in Gold. Charles II. (*c*) Braided Suit. 1670–90.

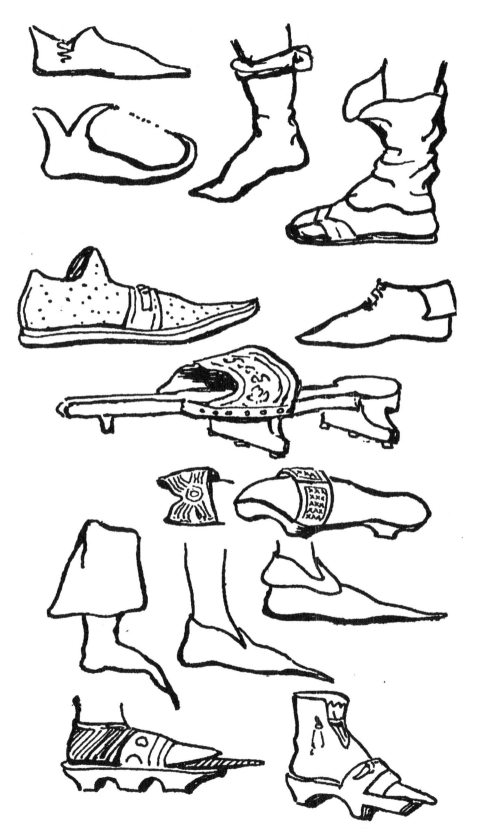

FIG. 35.—Fifteenth-century Shoes and Clogs.

The sleeves were now sometimes slit open at the back and held with several ties, as linen sleeves are now shown with these.

Parti-coloured tights were not so much favoured through this period, but a de-

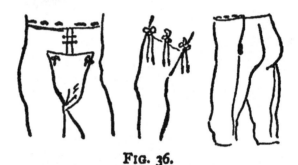

FIG. 36.

corated thigh, or part of the thigh and knee, was a favourite method of enrichment.

A long coat came in at the later part of this time, with a deep V-shaped collar meeting at the waist; it was also cut into a square shape at the shoulders, as in Fig. 43 (see p. 119). A loose bell-shaped sleeve usually went with this, often opened in the front of the upper arm. A short square cape is at times seen in conjunction with this. A low square or round neck shape came in during the last quarter of this century, filled in with a fine gathered lawn and a tight-fitting coat with a pleated

104

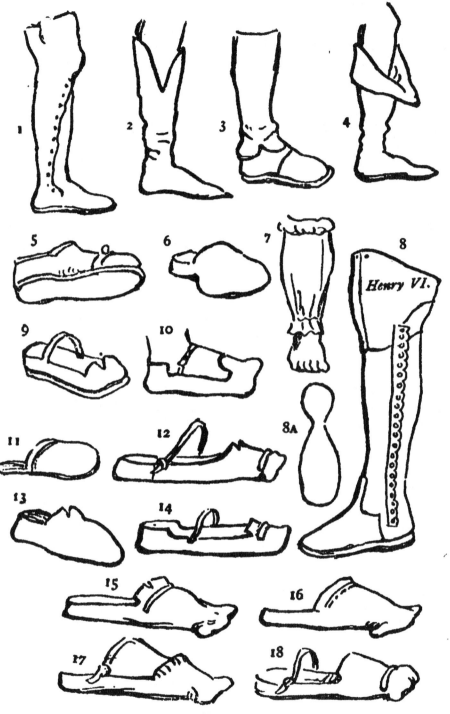

FIG. 37.

Nos. 1, 2, 3, 4, 5, 6, 7, 8, second half of 15th century.
Nos. 9, 10, 11, 12, 13, 14, 15, 16, 17, 18, variety of shapes from
1490 to 1630.

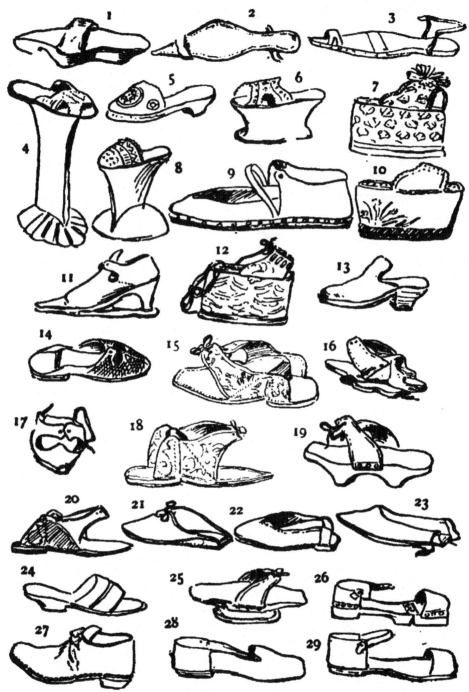

FIG. 38.

No.	No.	No.	No.
1. 14th century.	9. 1550–1600.	16. 1690–1720.	23. 1770–1800.
2. 15th century.	10. 1610–1640.	17. 1680–1700.	24. 1730–1760.
3. ,, ,,	11. 1590–1620.	18. 1700–1750.	25. 1700–1780.
4. Late 16th cent.	12. 1605–1630.	19. 1700–1780.	26. 1830–1860.
5. 1580–1610.	13. 1675–1695.	20. 1700–1760.	27. 1780–1800.
6. ,, ,,	14. 1670–1690.	21. 1740–1780.	28. 1840–1870.
7. 1605–1640.	15. 1680–1700.	22. 1745–1780.	29. ,, ,,
8. 1600–1625.			

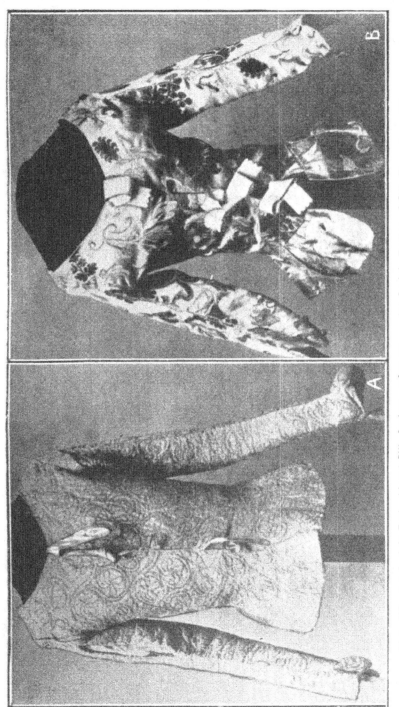

Plate IX.—(*a*) Lady's Embroidered Silk Jacket. 1605–30.   (*b*) Lady's Bodice of Silk Brocade. 1680–1700.

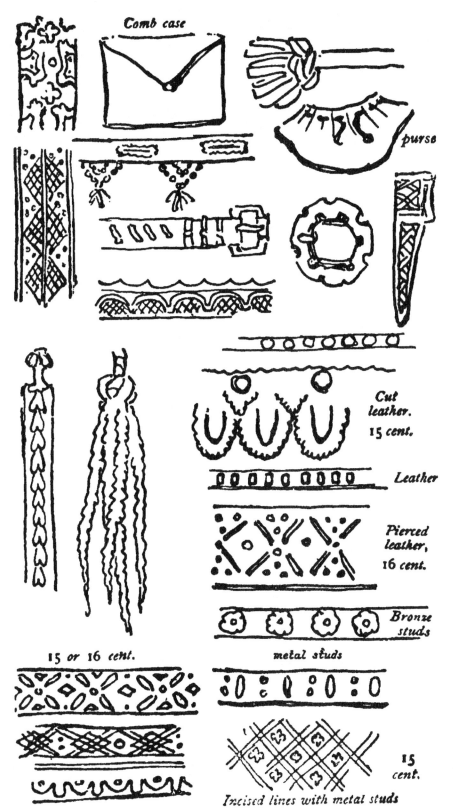

Comb case

purse

Cut leather. 15 cent.

Leather

Pierced leather. 16 cent.

Bronze studs

metal studs

15 or 16 cent.

15 cent.

Incised lines with metal studs

FIG. 39.—Decorated Leather, 15th and 16th centuries.

skirt and full padded sleeves, or a tight sleeve with a full puff or spherical upper part.

Shoes and boots were still worn with very long pointed toes till about 1465, when a proclamation was issued for beaks or piked shoes not to pass two inches, and after this time a broad round-toed shoe began to appear. Soft high boots to the top of the thigh, with folded top, belong to this century, as well as the fashionable boot to the calf. The sword or dagger was carried towards the front or side, and a small dagger across the belt at the back. The pouch or purse was also used as a dagger support.

CHAPTER V

SIXTEENTH CENTURY.   CHARACTER
OF TRIMMINGS.

BEFORE the 16th century we find the art
of decoration in costume had been con-
fined chiefly to applied ornamental bands
at the neck, waist, and borders of skirt and
cloak. They had up till this time utilised,
with great artistry of design (no doubt
partly due to the heraldic study), the
patterns of the finely decorated damasks
and velvets.   The counter colour effects
and relative proportions, such as a small-
patterned, dull-coloured silk setting off
a large full-coloured design was ably considered, as well as the introduction of a
nicely-balanced black note or setting, which
proved these designers were highly skilled
in judgment of style.   They also dis-
covered the art of giving enrichment and
lightness to the effect by means of the

109

various serrated edgings to the materials,
which also gave a flutter to the movement.
A preference of lacing for fastening added
to the charm of the dress, but the long
rows of close buttons were also a feature
of the clinging robes, the clasps and
brooches, neck-chains, girdle, belt, and
wallet being further very important items
of enrichment to the effect.

On coming to the 16th century we
enter what may be termed the slashed and
puffed period. The sleeves of Henry VIII's
reign are very rich in design and jewel-
setting, the design of the sleeve as in
Fig. 40 giving a striking effect, the angle
of the top sleeve being held out by the
stiffness of the under silk one. The
neck-setting and festooning of the jewel-
chains play an important part in the design
on the plain velvet corset bodices. The
head-dress is one of the most remarkable,
and gave a great chance for individual
arrangement in binding the back fall to
set at various angles on the shaped cap
piece, combining severity with a big loose
draping which is extremely picturesque.
With Edward VI commences what may be
termed the braided period of decoration.
This latter came suitably with the stiffer

110

corsage and set up. Mary's reign was not of attractive severity, but the over-robe with the short circular sleeve at the shoulder and high collar was a graceful creation, and was retained by many as late as 1630. There was little to admire in the Elizabethan age as regards design, except the beauty of the materials and the exquisite needlework. The proportions of the dresses were exceedingly ugly, and the pleated farthingale an absurdity. The male dress had much interest and often beauty of setting and decorative effect. The slashed materials gave a broken quality to what would otherwise be a hard effect, and it also cleverly introduced another colour change through the suit. There will be found many examples in these illustrations of the pricked and punctured designs on leather-work which are worth examining for modern treatment.

Quilting and pleating were ably combined with the braiding, and we see the clever adaptation of straw patterns sewn on (a feature of the late 16th century), which harmonised with the gold braidings or gold lace, or resembled the same effect.

The trimmings of braid were often enriched with precious or ornamental stones

and pearls, the stomacher, waist, front band
down the skirt, and borders of most garments. The points of slashes were often
held by jewelled settings, and the long
slashes were caught here and there with
the same.

Another important item was the black
stitchwork on linen, sometimes mingled
with gold, so highly prized now for its
beauty of design and effect, but beginning
probably in the reign of Henry VII.

Short coats of this type of the Elizabethan age are marvels of skill, and many
caps are still in existence. Fine linen ruffs
and collars were often edged with this
work, as well as with gold lace.

Jackets and caps, both male and female,
bearing geometrical and scroll designs in
gold, filled in with coloured needlework
of flowers, birds, or animals have happily
been preserved for our admiration.

Sequins appear on work from Henry
VIII's time, and were much appreciated
by the Elizabethan workers, who no doubt
found the trembling glitter added much
to the gold-lace settings and delicate veilings : long pear-shaped sequins were
favoured for this. Sleeves were often
separate, and could be changed at will.

The hair at this period was parted in the centre and gathered into a plait at the back; it was also seen rather full and waved at the sides of the head, and a small circlet was often carried across the brow. A cap of velvet or gold brocade, sometimes with a padded front, curved over the ears to the neck, keeping the shape of the head. Over this again a velvet fall was turned back from the front or shaped as in the illustration, reaching to the shoulder. These falls were also bound into set-out shapes, which gave many picturesque effects.

Dress had now taken a new phase, and the set bodice became a lasting feature. At this period the waist was rather short, and the neck, arranged in a low square or round form, generally filled in with gathered lawn. The upper part of the sleeve was often divided from the bodice by ties with lawn puffs, and was made in a full circular form, slashed or puffed and banded, with a tight-fitting sleeve on the forearm. Another type divided the upper and lower part of the arm at the shoulder

H   113

FIG. 40.—Sixteenth century, 2nd quarter.

Fig. 41.—Period Henry VIII.

and elbow, the forearm being effectively
tied or laced, and the under lawn sleeve
pulled through; small slashings are also
seen on these. At times a bell-shaped
sleeve was worn, showing a slashed or
puffed under one. Many dresses were still
cut in one, and were often high-necked;
with these usually a girdle or band of
drapery was worn, and some skirts opened
up the front, showing a rich underskirt.

Full skirts, heavily pleated at the waist,
were worn in the earlier part of this reign,
banded in varying widths of designs to
about the knee; but a new development
was in progress—a stiff, bell-shaped dress,
set on hoops over a rich underskirt which
usually bore a jewelled band down the
centre, the upper one being divided in
front to display this feature. The bodice
with this type becomes longer in the waist,
and was made on a stiff corset. Gloves
are occasionally seen, serrated at the cuff-
end. Shoes of the slashed character and
square toes were also worn by the ladies,
but many preferred a shoe with a moder-
ately rounded toe.

The first mention of a leather umbrella
is 1611, but this is a rare instance, as they
were not in use till the 18th century here,

116

FIG. 42.—Sixteenth-century modes, 1st half Henry VIII.

though they are noted in continental prints during the 17th century.

SIXTEENTH CENTURY. HENRY VIII.
MALE.

The modes at the end of the last century now developed into a heavier character of design. The long hair soon began to be closely cut, and a short beard came into fashion. A flat type of hat was worn, with serrated brim, or tabs which could be turned down at times, and others were kept in place by a lacing cord through holes. There was also a flat "Tam o' Shanter" shape, generally worn well tilted on one side, and amongst the upper classes mostly adorned with feathers.

The V-shaped collar, or opening to the belt, was still retained on the jerkin, and plain or pleated skirts are seen, also a square close-fitting vest, with a low square neck, filled with gathered lawn, or one with a high neck and short collar, on which a very small ruff appeared for the first time, and at the wrist as well. These were now decorated with long slashes or gathered puffs: heraldic design was still seen on the breast, and even parti-colour

118

Pattern, see p. 292.

Plate X.—(*a*) Black Velvet Bodice. 1600-25
(*b*) Five Embroidered Waistcoats. Between 1690 and 1800.

FIG. 43—Period Henry VIII.

Mask

FIG. 44.—Cap shapes. Period Henry VIII.

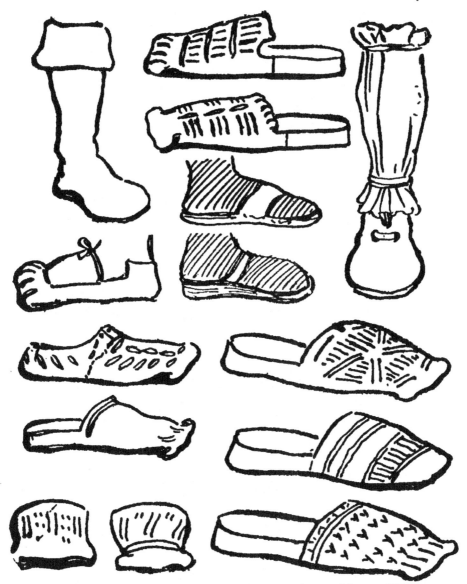

FIG. 45.—Variety of shapes and slashing.   Henry VIII.

was worn, but this character was now
treated more by decorating with coloured
bands on the tunics or tights.

Long coats were still worn of the shape
described at the end of the 15th century,
but a short surcoat was the mode, reaching
just below the knee, sleeveless, or with the
various hanging sleeves of this period, the
fronts usually turned back to form a wide
collar, either round or square in shape on
the shoulder, or at times falling to a deep
square at the back.

The sleeves were full in the upper part,
tightening to the wrist, sometimes open up
to the elbow and laced, or they were pleated
into a full round shape at the shoulder.
Puffs and slashings increased in these designs, and by 1520 we find the sleeves
mostly divided into puffed and slashed
forms, which grew to fantastic proportions.

Very short, tight breeches or trunks, with
a front flap or codpiece, were decorated to
match the body design and colour schemes;
they increased in length to the knee, or
just below, during this reign, and usually
finished in a serrated roll.

Shoes were of the square form, some very
short in front, held on by a strap across
the instep, others with fronts to the instep.

1. 1740-1780.
2. 1535-1550.
3. 1680-1700.
4. 1645-1680.
5. 1665-1685.
6. 1690-1710.
7. 1845-1860.
8. 1790-1820.
9. 1665-1670.
10. 1800-1820.
11. 1820-1810.
12. „
13. 1815-1850.
14. 1760-1780.
15. 1650-1670.
16. 1630-1660.

Plate XI.—16 Leather Boots and shoes. Between 1535 and 1860.

Toe portions of Shoes

FIG. 46.—Footwear, 1510–1540.

The corners were often brought out to a point on each side of the toes, and the mode of decorating with slashing and punctures made them very interesting. The sides of these shoes are very low, from $\frac{3}{4}$ to 1 inch, and no heels are seen. A big, round shape was also favoured, which increased in width till a proclamation forbade it exceeding 6 inches. Chains were still a decorative feature round the neck, and the belt carried a sword and pouch, or, amongst the working classes, other necessities.

SIXTEENTH CENTURY. THE REIGNS OF EDWARD VI AND MARY. FEMALE.

Sixteenth
Century.
The Reigns
of
Edward VI
and Mary.
Female.

In the reign of Edward VI, which was so short, as also in that of Mary, there was little time to form a real character. These reigns form developing links to the Elizabethan era, so I have taken them in one chapter.

With Edward VI the same shaped cap is seen as that of Henry VIII, and with Mary's accession, the head-dress is curved to the head in a like manner, but it now became more of a hat form and took a brim curved in on the brow; this was

FIG. 47.

FIG. 48.

FIG. 49

Elizabethan modes.

FIG. 50.—Costumes, 1554–1568.

FIG. 51.—Costumes, 1568–1610.

Sixteenth
Century.
The Reigns
of
Edward VI
and Mary.
Female

often worn over the little tight curved
cap, or showed the hair waved out at the
sides, often netted with gold and pearls.
A fall of velvet, silk, or veiling was still
retained till the very high ruff or collar
came in the Elizabethan days. A small-
crowned hat, with a brooch and feather
in front, and a full gathered crown came
in before Elizabeth's time, when we see
many eccentric shapes, such as the tall hat
with a feather at the side, and the witch-
like hats towards the end of her reign.

The bodice, which became longer in the
first reign, still retained the full belled oversleeve or the full puffed sleeve to the end
of Mary's reign, also the same square
neck shape with curved-up front, now
often filled with silk quilted with pearls
up to the neck. High-necked dresses
set with a small ruff became general in
Mary's reign. We also find a tight sleeve
gathered in a circular puff at the shoulder
or set in a rolled epaulet.

The same shaped skirt of the hooped
bell form (sometimes very pleated in Mary's
reign) or divided in front to show the underskirt as described under Henry VIII, was
worn.

The short square shape and the heavy

128

round shoe is seen in Mary's reign, but fashion then preferred a rather pointed oval shoe, well up the instep with higher sides, decorated with characteristic slashing. Gloves are seen in many portraits up to this period, but of a plain make minus embroidery, and a circular fan of feathers was carried.

SIXTEENTH CENTURY. THE REIGNS OF EDWARD VI AND MARY. MALE.

With Edward VI and Mary a more refined and sober type of style set in. The hair was now worn short and combed backwards. The flat hat of the earlier shapes lasted to Elizabeth's reign; becoming smaller in width, with a turned-down, curved brim and a fuller crown encircled with a gold band or set with a feather worn at the right-hand side. A small tight-fitting round hat with a rolled brim and a feather in front is also of this later mode. Through these reigns a small square turned-over collar or a very small ruff set on a high collar came into use, which increased to a larger ruff in Mary's reign. A small ruff was also worn at the wrist, many of these were

Fig. 43.—Costumes, 1575-1580.

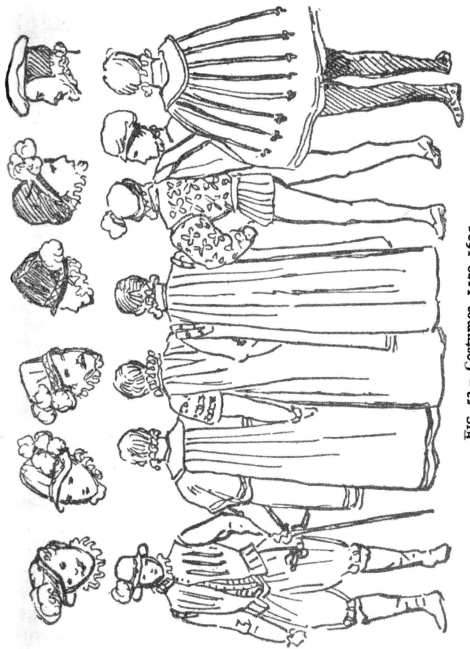

FIG. 53.—Costumes, 1570–1605.

Sixteenth
Century.
The Reigns
of
Edward VI
and Mary.
Male

edged with black-stitch designs. The
heavy puffed sleeves became tight and
started from a small epaulet or puffed
roll; some of these had a small cuff at the
wrist or a frill. Braided designs became
very elaborate on a close-fitting, padded,
and round-shaped jerkin with a short
skirt, which appeared in the first reign,
and this skirt was often long enough to
fasten just under the codpiece. Short
trunks at times worn half-way down the
thigh were slashed, banded, and puffed
for decoration. No parti-colour was now
worn or striped effects on tights, except
amongst the soldiers in the reign of Mary.
Short capes to the length of the trunks
of a plain round form sloping from the
shoulders, or a square type with a high
square collar and loose sleeves, are seen;
a tunic also of the earlier character with
a V-shaped collar and full sleeve comes
into this reign, and we note the earlier
types of shoes mingling with the newer
pointed oval-shaped shoe which now continued for the remainder of this century.

In Mary's reign the round-shaped doublet
began to protrude from the breast to the
waist in a round form with slightly longer
skirts or small tabs, while the trunks

132

assumed large circular proportions and were sometimes set on tight knee-breeches. The capes remained about the same.

SIXTEENTH CENTURY. ELIZABETH. FEMALE.

The costly splendour of attire is well known in Elizabeth's reign, which began with the same form of hair and head-dress as with Mary, the hat being set rather higher on the hair. The ruffs, which were imported already starched from Holland, assumed larger proportions and complications when the methods of starching became known in England about 1564. Stow describes ruffs growing to a quarter of a yard deep; these were no doubt supported by piccalilloes, though they are not actually mentioned till after 1600, but they surely came with the fan-shaped structures of these later days. White, red, blue or purple colours were used in the starching, and yellow in the latter days of this century. The introduction of this curved fanlike collar setting became a grand and complicated feature right into the 17th century. "Make up" became very apparent on the faces at this time,

133

FIG. 54.—Elizabethan modes.

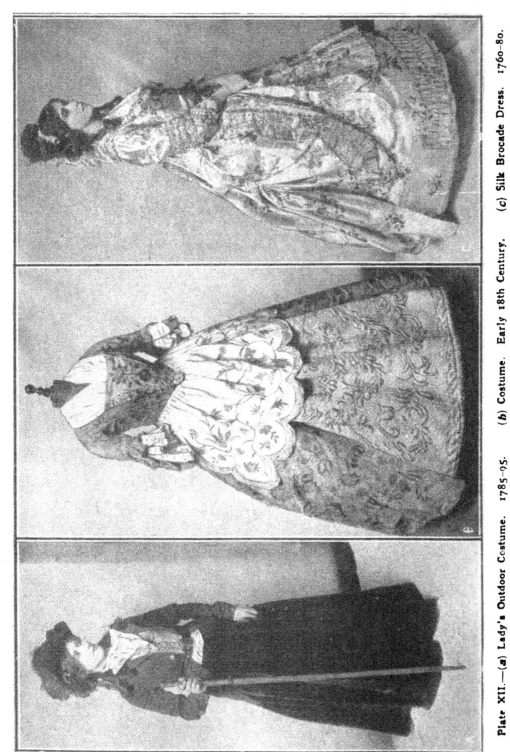

Plate XII.—(*a*) Lady's Outdoor Costume. 1785-95.   (*b*) Costume. Early 18th Century.   (*c*) Silk Brocade Dress. 1760-80.

1589-1600

1605-15

1595-1605

FIG. 55.

1600-1620

1585-1610

for Bishop Hall censured the fashion in a choice sermon, saying, "Hear this, ye plaster-faced Jezabels! God will one day wash them with fire and brimstone."

The bodices grew very long and pointed in the waist, the neck setting being mostly treated in the same V shape, even open down to the waist point was filled with a decorated stomacher, and a deep oval-shaped neck was seen at the end of the reign. An outer opened sleeve was now favoured, caught in front at the elbow and hanging to the knee over a fairly tight under-sleeve with a turned-back lace cuff or ruffle. With this came the high-set fan ruff on its wooden support at the back of the neck, and consequently a higher coiffure.

The same character of skirt continued as in the earlier reigns on hoops at the lower part, but they became much fuller and rounder at the hips till about 1590, when the full pleated skirt was supported on a farthingale or hoop which was set with a gathered circle in the same goffered design as the ruffs at the edge. These reached their extreme dimensions at the end of this reign, when the sleeves also assumed a full padded shape and large

136

FIG. 56.

Nos. 1, 2, 3, 1540-50, and other shoe forms worn in the reign of Elizabeth.

epaulets also came in. An overdress with a full pleated back (like the Watteau dress) was in fashion from the middle of this reign, and we are lucky to possess some specimens in the Victoria and Albert Museum of which I am able to give the dimensions. Small looking-glasses were carried, and were also inset on the round feather fans. Perfumed gloves, elaborately embroidered, were introduced during this reign. Silk stockings were worn by Elizabeth for the first time in 1560, and worsted stockings were made in England in 1564. Corsets of pierced steel are seen in France from the late 16th and 17th century, and may have been in use here, though wood, cane, and whalebone were the chief supports. Shoes became narrow and even pointed, while the heel began to increase to considerable heights. The buskins of Queen Elizabeth now at Oxford are raised to 3 inches in height by the aid of a thick sole, and shoes A and B, Fig. 61, are also reported to have belonged to her. Chopins for heightening the stature were in use on the Continent, but I believe did not appear here; but very thick corked soles and high heels were introduced for this purpose.

138

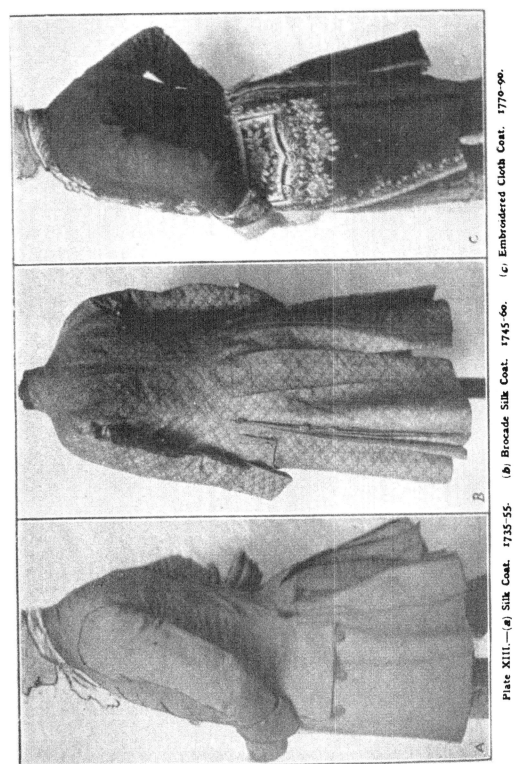

Plate XIII.—(a) Silk Coat. 1735–55.   (b) Brocade Silk Coat. 1745–60.   (c) Embroidered Cloth Coat. 1770–90.

SIXTEENTH CENTURY. ELIZABETH. MALE.

In this reign a very neat small-pointed beard was the fashion, the hair being brushed up as high as possible and often fulled out at the sides, and a "chic" appearance was sought after. A stiff belled top-hat with an egret at the right side made its first appearance with a curved brim, also one of a tapered shape with a smallish round brim, and another very small round hat with a curved brim, a clasp and feather being mostly worn on the front of each. The brims of all the hats began to enlarge at the end of the century, when the very high crowned wide brimmed hat made its appearance, sometimes with a peaked top, and beaver is first mentioned in their make.

Large circular ruffs became all the rage besides the small turned-over collar. The round doublet with protruding front became tighter at the waist, the protuberance taking a punchlike pointed form curving to almost between the legs and sloping sharply up the hips to the back. This was set with a very short tab or tabs on

139

padded breeches tightening to the knee, which usually had very small trunks on the upper part, and large, stuffed trunk hose also appeared. The stockings were brought over these in a roll above the knee. Up to this time tights were made of wool, worsted, fine cloth, frieze, and canvas. The slashings, pleating, and gatherings of the period were of a much neater character, and punched patterns and pricked materials came into use.

Close-fitting high boots, generally with serrated tops and thick soles curving into a short heel, are features of this time. The shoe had a long front decorated with slashings (often caught with jewels), and an oval toe which became almost pointed in the last years of this century. A short top-boot rising to the calf was also in use, mostly with a little fur edge at the top, and these were often pricked with patterns.

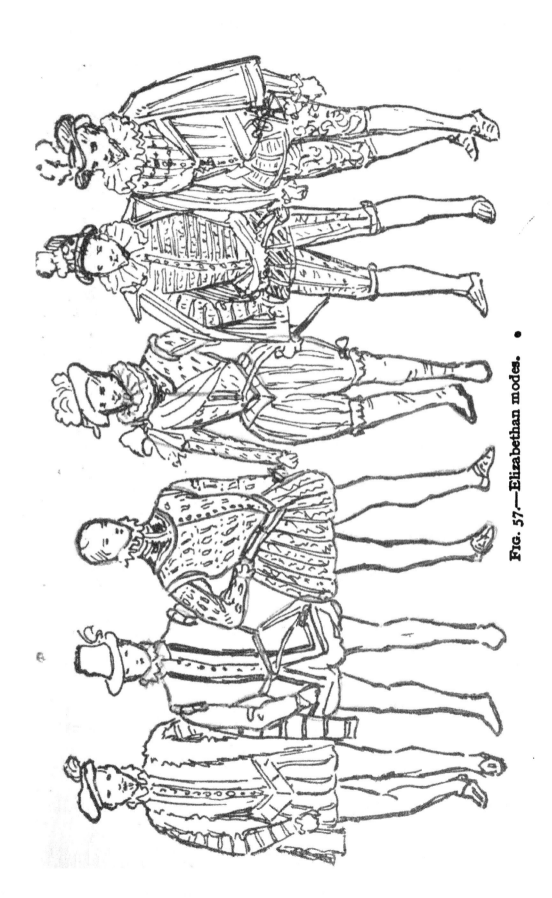

FIG. 57.—Elizabethan modes.

CHAPTER VI

THE CHARACTER OF TRIMMINGS THROUGH THE SEVENTEENTH CENTURY.

JAMES I.

The Charac-
ter of
Trimmings
through the
Seventeenth
Century.
James I
THE braiding and small slashing continued of a similar character to the end of the Elizabethan age. The slashing now began to be treated with a larger effect and less elaboration, but pricking and punching were still much used for enriching surfaces. An improved style of design was evident.

The female bodice was arranged with a long stomacher, often shaped into curved forms at the point, and this was set with jewels or embroidery, otherwise the bodice was decorated with braiding and jewels as in Elizabeth's reign. The full sleeves were embellished with small slashes (making diamond squares), puffs, or

142

pricked and punched designs. A turned-up cuff or ruff of pointed lace finished the wrist, braided epaulets formed a beautiful feature of the effect, and the front of the underskirt was decorated with a jewelled band or conventional design, as was also the border of the overskirt. Caps of an interesting curved form beautifully embroidered in gold and coloured silks are seen, of which I give patterns; also loose jackets of the same work were in use when not in full dress.

The Charac-
ter of
Trimmings
through the
Seventeenth
Century.
James I

CHARLES I.

Many beautifully embroidered caps, jerkins, jackets, and shirts are seen at this period in gold and black or coloured silks. Slashings of this reign, though in fashion, had commenced to go out; and those retained were of a large character, mostly from the neck or shoulder to the breast. The favoured sleeves were cut into straps to the elbow or wrist, and were often edged with braid, either side meeting together and lining the forearm, the body being treated in the same way. The open-fronted sleeve was set with buttons

143

The Charac-
ter of
Trimmings
through the
Seventeenth
Century.
Charles I

and loops or long braided buttonholes with frayed or knotted ends, though these were not generally fastened. The tight undersleeve was often set with gold or silver narrow braids down the front and back seams, and close lines of small braids horizontally round the arm, or vertically when the outer sleeve was treated horizontally, this gave a beautiful counterchanged effect.

Many of the ladies' caps of this time had beautiful gold scrolls, with flowers and birds embroidered in coloured silks, also loose jackets of the same were in use. The bodice was banded with braids or lace on the front and seams, and the stomacher was often of fine embroidery; set rosettes or bows were placed at the waist. Other finishing effects of collar or sleeve, and the button and buttonhole decorations were made important features on both male and female sleeves, and even down the front of the outer skirt when it was not treated with lace. Red heels to shoes began to be worn and continued to the end of the 18th century in marked favour.

During this short period the character and placing of braiding was the same as in the latter part of last reign; slashing had almost completely gone out, except for the treatment of some ladies' sleeves cut into bands. A very sober effect was assumed in colour schemes, besides a plainer treatment in decoration, and a deep plain collar or a small turn-over one was chiefly worn by the men, while the hat of the Puritan rose to an absurd height, with a wide flat brim.

The Character of Trimmings through the Seventeenth Century. The Commonwealth

CHARLES II.

This may be named the period of ribbon trimmings, though braiding was treated in broad lines on the short jackets and sleeves, and down the sides of the breeches. A preference is shown for gold and silver lace, or amongst the élite purfled silk edges; the new mode being a decoration of groups of ribbon loops placed about the suit or dress. The notable feature with the female dress was the gathering of drapery by means of jewelled clasps, and groups of ribbon loops were also used,

Charles II

K 145

The Charac-
ter of
Trimmings
through the
Seventeenth
Century.
Charles II
as with the male dress. The edges of the
materials were sometimes cut into scalloped
or classic forms, and a very simple volumi-
nous character was fashion's aim.

JAMES II AND WILLIAM AND MARY.

With the later type of long-skirted coat
which began in Charles II's reign, a heavy
style of braiding and buttoning came into
vogue, all the seams of the coat besides the
pockets and cuffs and fronts being braided,
which fashion continued to the end of
the century. Many coats began to be
embroidered in the later reign, and waistcoats became a special feature for the
display of fine needlecraft on the fronts
and pockets, while quilting or imitations
of it in various needlework designs are
often seen. In the female dress a more
elaborate interest was again taken in the
stomachers and the jewelled claspings,
while lengths of soft silk gathered into
long puffs often edged the outer skirts or
were used in smaller trimmings, and "classi-
cal" shapings of the edges of materials and
sleeves are often seen, also heavy bands
of rich embroidery bordered the underskirt or train.

We find much the same high forms of set-up head-dress continuing in fashion as in the later years of Elizabeth's reign; but the hair began to take a fuller shape, rather round, done up in tight frizzled curls, with the usual decorations of jewels, pearls, or set bows of this period. Hats with high crowns and small straight brims, with an upright set of small plumes, gradually assumed a larger brimmed character—often turned up on one side. The same absurd pleated hoop, with its hanging skirt, continued for some time (worn rather short); but we also see the longer and very full hooped-out skirt, with an overskirt opened in the front. The stomacher front became much enlarged during this reign, many having shaped designs at the point. Most bodices took a very deep curved front at the neck, and large padded sleeves narrowed at the wrist still continued, besides the high fan collar at the back of the neck, and large ruffs were used by many. There also appeared, later in the reign, a stiff round collar, set high in the neck, cut off straight across

147

1610-30

1610-25

1590-1610

1600-1615

FIG. 58.

FIG. 59.—Costumes. Period, James I.

the front, and the bodice took a very low square-cut neck, with a raised curved shape at the centre of neck. The tighter sleeve was also worn throughout this time, with the overdress and sleeve hanging almost to the ground, which often had a very angular cuff. A little later some sleeves began to be gathered at intervals into puffy forms. The waist also showed signs of shortening.

Shoes with rounded toes and latchets holding large rosettes were chiefly worn, and heels of various heights are seen. Chopins, still worn on the Continent, do not seem to have appeared here.

SEVENTEENTH CENTURY. JAMES I.
MALE.

The hat was of the high-crowned type, perhaps higher than in the last reign. The brim had broadened, and feathers were placed upwards fantastically at the back and sides of crown. Brims were often fastened up on the right side with a jewel; otherwise a band was buckled in front. The hair was now allowed to fall longer again, and a pointed or square-shaped beard with a brushed-up moustache was the mode. Ruffs both large and small surrounded the

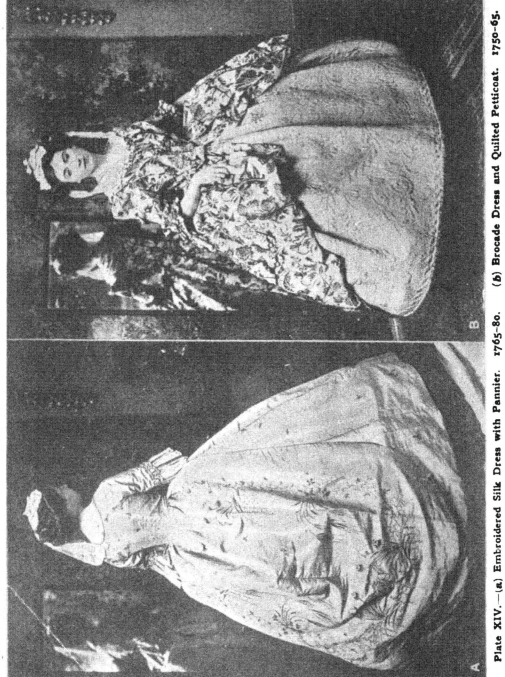

Plate XIV.—(*a*) Embroidered Silk Dress with Pannier. 1765–80. (*b*) Brocade Dress and Quilted Petticoat. 1750–65.

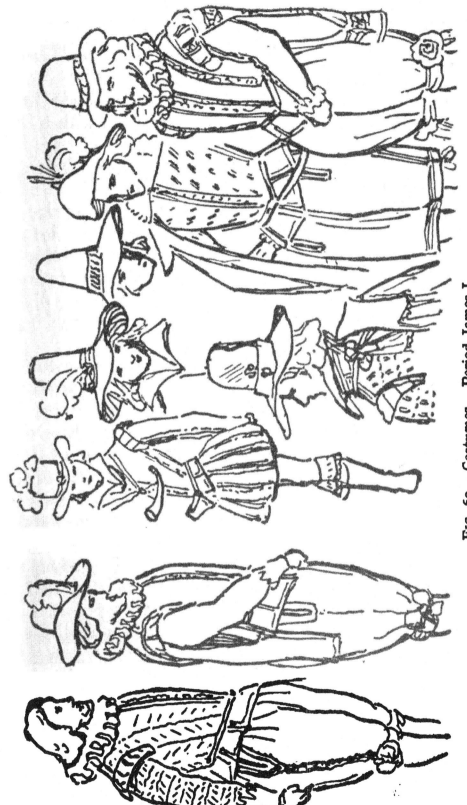

FIG. 60.—Costumes. Period James I.

neck, and a flat fan-shaped collar was seen in the earlier years.

The jerkin was close fitting and the length of the waist more normal, with less tendency to being tightened in, and not so deep in the front point, so as to set better over the very full trunks or breeches. The square tabs of the jerkin increased in size, and soon formed large flaps divided into three or four, to the centre of the back. Sleeves were fairly tight and started from slightly larger epaulets, and were usually set at the wrist, either with a small ruff or turned-up lawn cuff, edged with lace.

The trunks were padded in a very full shape and were much longer, just above the knee. Also full padded-out breeches tapering to the knee or just above, where a large tie and bow hung at the side, and full square breeches not tied in, are also a feature of these days, usually banded with wide braids at ends and sides. Upright pockets were made on either side towards the front, about two inches from the side seams. They fastened up the front in a pleated fold, many being decorated with punched, pricked, or slashed design of a smallish character.

Cloaks were worn longer to the knee,

152

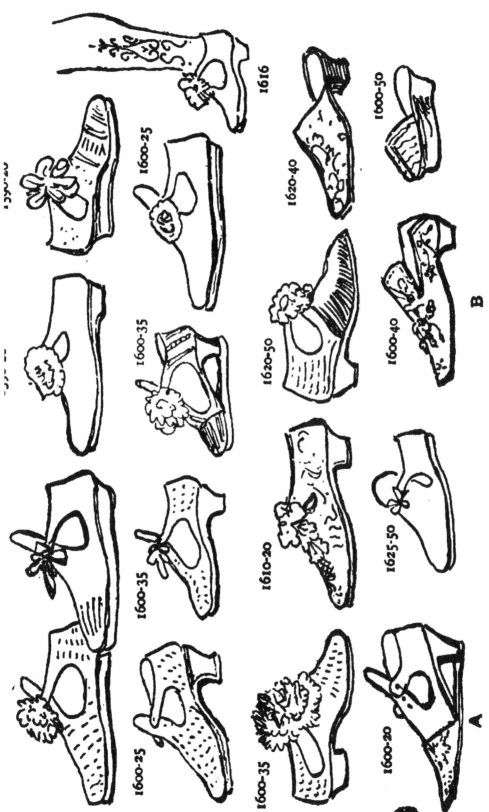

1616

1600-25

1620-40

1600-50

1600-35

1620-50

1600-40

B

1600-35

1610-20

1625-50

1600-25

1600-35

1600-20

A

Fig. 61.—Shapes of Shoes from 1590–1650.

retaining the same shapes and braid decoration as in the Elizabethan period, and hanging sleeves were still worn on them, as well
as on some of the jerkins.

Shoes became fuller and rounder at the
toes, mostly with thick welted soles and
short heels, or none. They were fastened
with a large rosette of gold lace or ribbon
on the front, and the latchets were set back
to show an open side. The top-boots were
close fitting and took squarer toes; the
spur flap being rather small. Beautifully
embroidered clocks are seen on the tights
and stockings of this period.

SEVENTEENTH CENTURY. CHARLES I.
FEMALE.

The hair was now allowed to fall in
ringlets round the back and sides, with a
few flat curls on the brow, and a bow and
pearls were caught in at the sides. Short
feathers may also be noted in use. A plait
was often coiled at the back after 1630.

In the early part of this reign the ladies
were wearing the long corset-bodice, with a
richly decorated stomacher which curved
outwards to set on the very full skirts;
this often finished with a curved or foliated

154

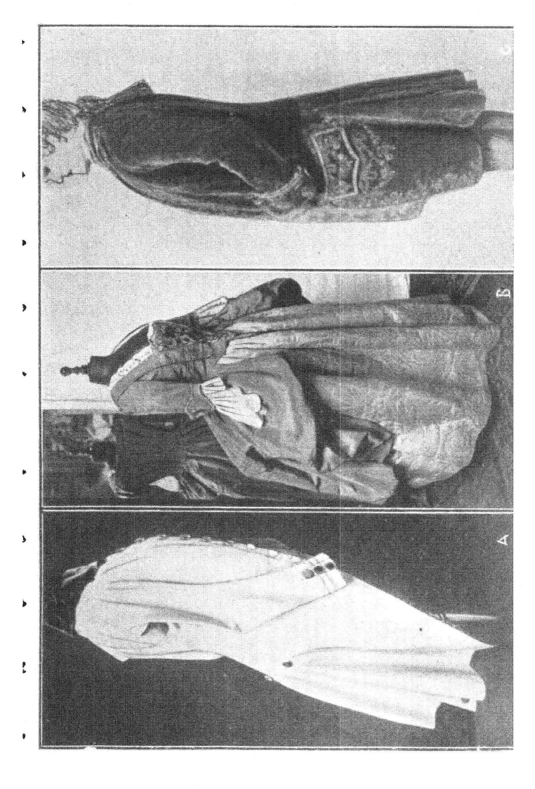

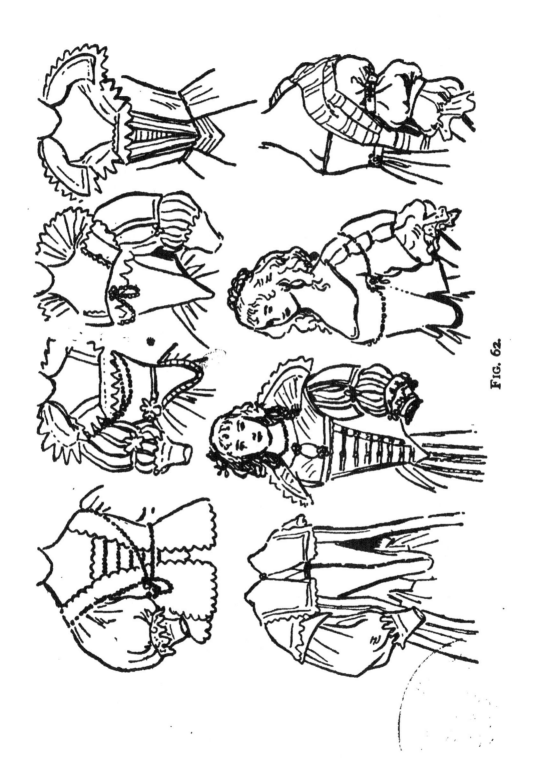

FIG. 62.

FIG. 63.

Collar and Bodice types. Period Charles I.

FIG. 64.
Collar and Bodice types.   Period Charles I to 1660.

shape at the point. Square starched collars,
rounded at the back, sometimes set up at
the back of the neck or flat on the shoulder,
and ruffs were still seen round the neck
with collars as well, but they were seldom
met with after 1635. A plainer, deep
collar, flat, round, or V-shaped at the back,
coming well over the shoulders, was caught
together by a bow or ornament in front.
About 1630 shorter waisted bodices came
in, with full, loose sleeves set in epaulets:
the neck shape was rounded or square.
The bodices were often slashed, and the
full sleeves, cut into bands, were sometimes
gathered by cross bands from one to three
times. Full plain sleeves, opened in the
front seam, were also clasped at the elbow
in a like manner. Outer short sleeves
became a feature, opening in the front,
showing the full under one or a tight one;
the waist became very short and its tabs
larger. A waistband fastened in the stomacher with a bow either side and bows
with long gold tags decorated the waist
as in the male jerkin. The skirt decorated
by a band of ornament down the front
was often tied upon the corset-bodice, the
front point being left outside. Shoes of
the same shape as the male illustrations,

158

FIG. 65.—Period 1625–1660.

with very square toes, were frequent, but an oval toe, rather pointed, is seen in many pictures, with the large lace rosettes in front. Muffs are first noticed in these days, though they were seen much earlier on the Continent.

SEVENTEENTH CENTURY. CHARLES I.
MALE.

The hair was worn loose to the shoulders, and a small plait was sometimes arranged on the left side, brought to the front of shoulder. The beard was trimmed to a pointed shape, and smarter curled moustaches were fashionable. Hats were still high in the crown, but rather lower than with James I; the large brims were turned about in various curves, and feathers were worn falling over the brims to the side or back.

The jerkin was high in the collar, supporting a large, square, turn-down collar edged with pointed lace to the shoulders, or a small, plain, turn-over collar; ruffs are very rarely seen after 1630.

A rather short waist grew shorter during this reign, with much larger tabs, or large flaps laced to the body, forming a series of bows with long gilt tags round the waist.

160

FIG. 66.—Charles I.

L

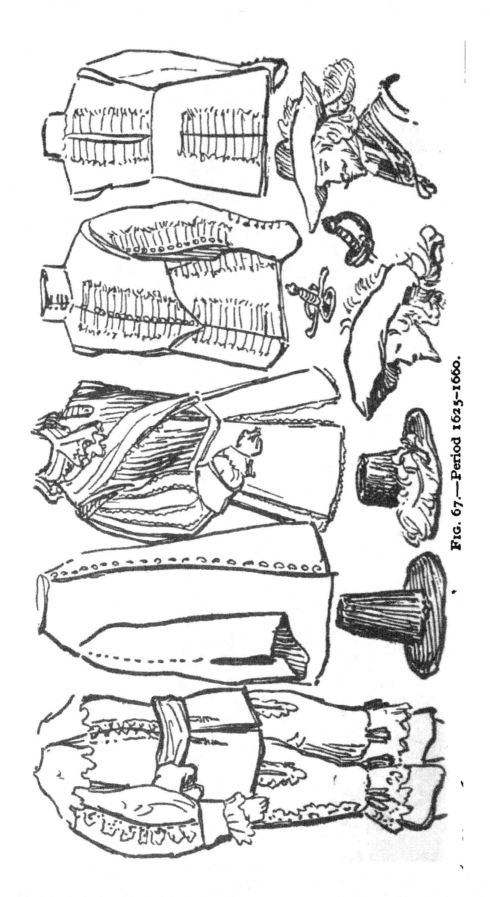

FIG. 67.—Period 1625-1660.

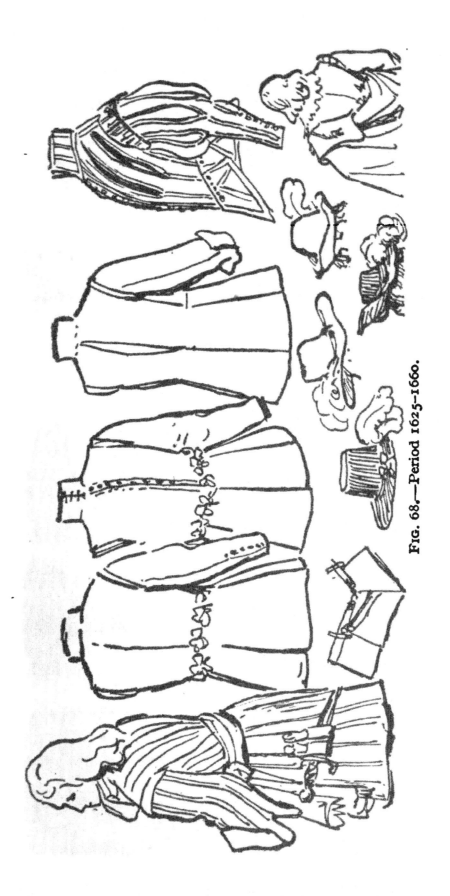

FIG. 68.—Period 1625-1660.

The body is usually decorated with long slashes from the shoulders to the breast, or the full length, and a long slashed opening is often seen in the back (presumably to give more play to the sword-thrust). The sleeve is also treated in the same way to the elbow or waist. All sleeves start from a stiff epaulet. Breeches are both very full and fairly tight, the latter edged with a purfling of silk or gold lace as well as the sides, the former shape tied either above or below the knee with a large silk bow with falling ends. They were held up by a number of hooks, fastening to a small flap with eyelets, round the inside of the doublet (see pattern 11, p. 295), and were buttoned down the front, the buttons being half hidden in a pleat. The pockets were placed vertically in the front of the thigh, and were frequently of a decorative character.

A short or long circular cloak was worn, and a coat-cloak with opened sleeves is an interesting garment. These coverings were hung in various ways from the shoulders by methods of tying the cords across the body.

Shoes became very square at the toes, or blocked as in Fig. 70, No. 6. The fronts

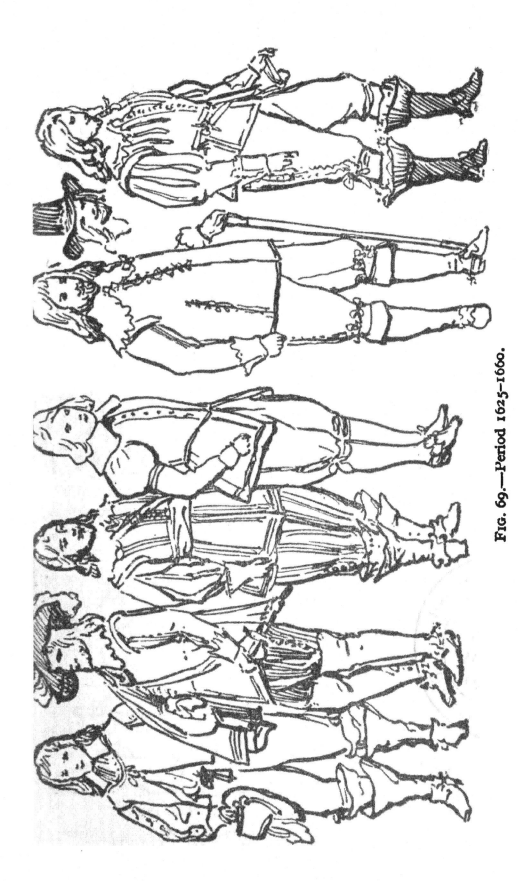

FIG. 69.—Period 1625–1660.

FIG. 70.—Shoe shapes.   Charles I to 1700.

Nos. 1, 2, 3, 4, 5, 6, 7, 8, 23.   Charles I.
Nos. 9, 10, 11, 12, 13, 14, 15, 16, 17, 25.   Charles II.
Nos. 18, 19, 20, 21, 22, 24, 26, 27, 28.   James II and William and Mary.

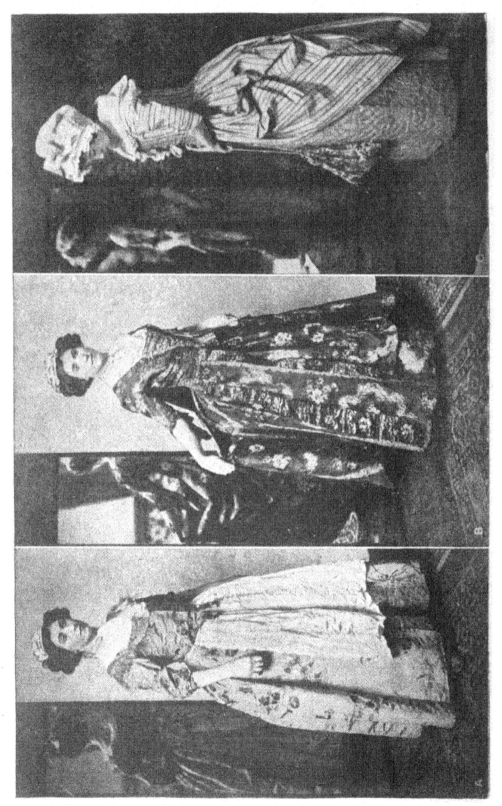

Plate XVI.—(*a*) Silk Brocade Dress. 1740–60.   (*b*) Silk Brocade Sack-back Dress. 1755–75.   (*c*) Dress of Striped Material. 1775–85.

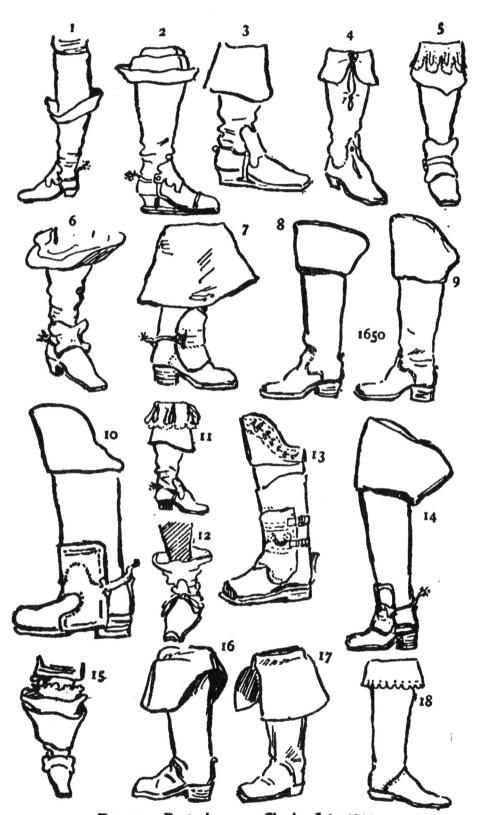

FIG. 71.—Boot shapes.   Charles I to 1700.

Nos. 1, 2, 3, 4, 5, 6, 7, 8, 9. Charles I.

Nos. 10, 11, 12, 13, 14, 15. Charles II.

Nos. 16, 17, 18.   James II and William and Mary.

were set with large rosettes of silk and
silver or gold lace, the heels varied much
in height, that mostly favoured being a
large, low heel. A quaint fashion of shoe
combined with a clog sole was an interesting shape (see illustration of clogs, p. 106).
Fairly tight top-boots, coming well above
the knee, were often turned down. Other
boots with large bell-tops, turned over or
pushed down, were covered or filled with
a lace or bell-shaped stocking-top. A
sash was worn round the waist or across
the body over the left shoulder (the length
and width of these is given in the description of patterns, p. 279). A broad belt,
or sword-hanger, came across the right
shoulder. Gloves were beautifully embroidered in gold, pearls, or coloured silks,
the gauntlets being from five to eight
inches deep.

SEVENTEENTH CENTURY. THE COMMON-WEALTH. MALE AND FEMALE.

Seventeenth
Century.
The
Common-
wealth.
Male and
Female The same shapes apply to costume during
the Commonwealth, though a sterner effect
was given by the choice of plain decoration
and less colour. A small or a large plain
collar, and the disappearance of slashings

168

on the coat, and a longer skirt became noticeable. A very high tapered hat, with stiff circular brim, was worn by the Puritans, and little, close, black hoods were much favoured. A general reaction from gay extravagance set in.

SEVENTEENTH CENTURY.   CHARLES II.
FEMALE.

The hair was set out from the head on combs with falling ringlets, and several small flat ringlets were placed on the forehead. The back of the hair was plaited into a knot, and pearl strings were interlaced, or ribbon loops caught in at either side. Toward 1680 the hair was worn tightly curled and fulled out into a round shape with a curl or two falling on the front of the shoulders; small feathers or long feathers were also worn. Hats were of a similar shape to those of the last reign, with a stiffer and narrower curved brim; but the chief head-dress was a large hood faced with another material, which latter was tied under the chin; these mostly formed part of a cape also.

The bodice again became much longer and of a pointed shape, but many corset bodices took a round point, and a round

FIG. 72.—Period 1650–1685.

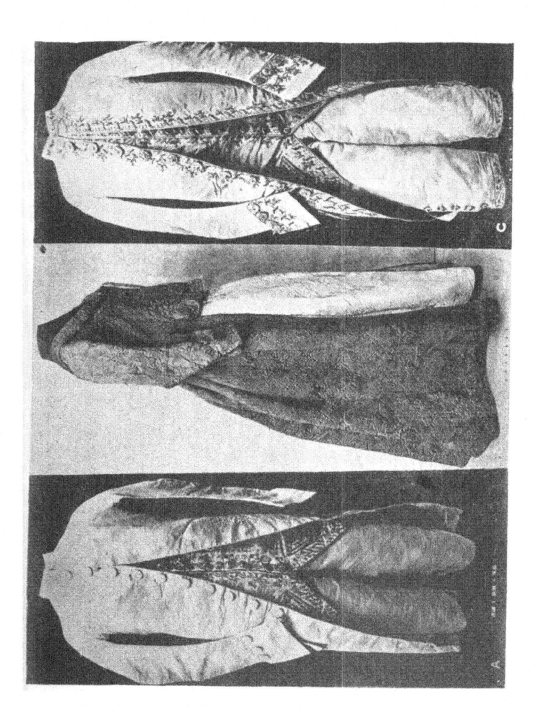

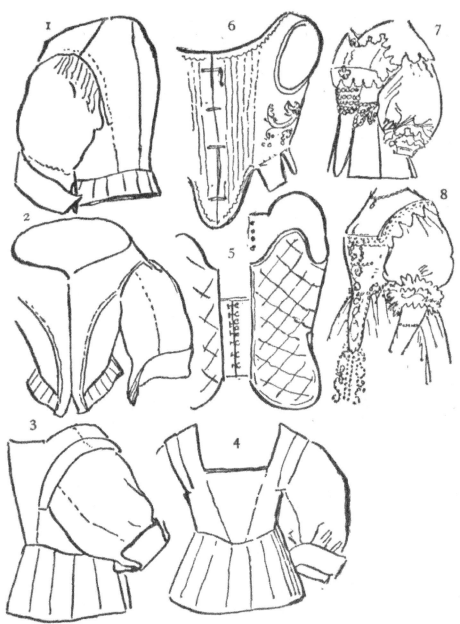

FIG. 73.

1, 2, 3, 4.—Back and Front of two Corset Bodices. Period Charles II.
5, 6.—Two Corsets. Period Charles II.
7, 8.—Two Bodice types. Period Charles I.

neck coming well off the shoulders became
general, usually decorated with a plain wide
band of lace. Ruffs and collars were no
longer seen amongst the upper classes.
Very full sleeves and large opened sleeves
were tied or clasped over full lawn ones, and
at times separated from the shoulders, being
caught effectively with jewels. Groups of
ribbons were placed at the breast or point
of the bodice, and the ends of sleeves or
shoulders, besides at the fronts of the outer
skirt when divided, also in the gathering of
the lawn sleeves. Stomachers were not much
worn, but a drape of soft silk was caught
here and there round the neck of bodice, and
large draperies were clasped to the shoulders.
Loose robes and robes shaped to the figure,
opening down the front from the neck
even to the waist, with a clasp or several
holding them together; these were worn over
a quilted linen corset laced in front as in
the illustration, but the bodice was often
formed on a corset. Long gloves and
mittens were in use, and small muffs with
ribbon loops on the front were carried.
High-heeled shoes with very long square
toes were affected in imitation of the male
shoe, but most ladies now began to wear
a very pointed shoe.

172

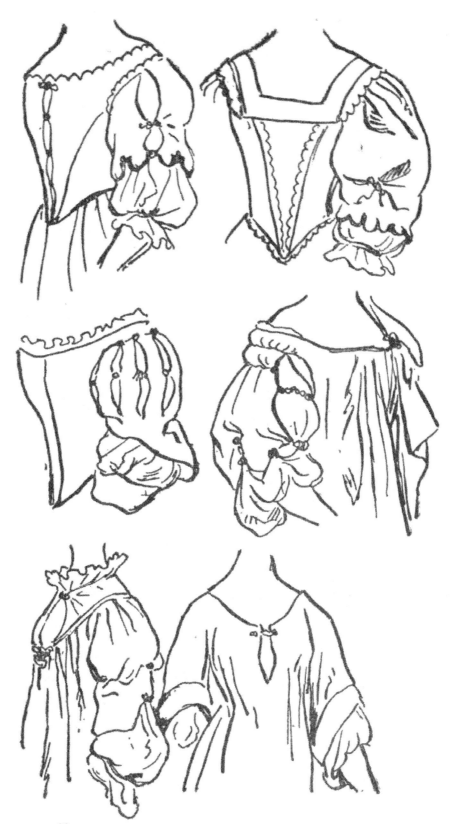

FIG. 74.—Sleeve treatments.   Period Charles II.

Long hair or wigs of long curls falling on the shoulders, a very narrow moustache and point of beard on the chin came with this reign. Lace collars of a smaller square or rounded shape were in use, but a fall of lace pleated in the centre soon took its place. High-crowned hats with a band and bow in front and a flat, waved, or curved brim, with feathers on either side or all round, were the fashion, the crowns becoming shorter during the reign; the fronts and sometimes the sides of the brim are seen turned up, and so begins to form the three-cornered hat, which remained so long a feature in history.

We find with extravagant shapes a happy return of gay colours. The high-waisted jerkins of the Charles I period were now seen without the skirt (as very short jackets), leaving the lawn shirt to show between this and the breeches, besides which the jackets were nearly always left unbuttoned several inches up, some being cut away in a rounded shape and also having short sleeves. The lower arm was

174

FIG. 75.—Period Charles II.

covered with a full lawn sleeve caught at
two or even three distances with a loop
of ribbons or bows, and finishing with a
wide lace frill; a bunch of ribbon loops was
also often seen on the right shoulder. A
long circular cloak, with turned-back fronts
forming a collar in many, still retained the
hanging sleeve, and was mostly decorated
with bands of heavy braid. A long square
coat also came in about 1666, buttoned right
down the front, with pockets set very low
in the skirt, and large narrow cuffs opened
at the back as in Plate VIII (see p. 90).

Very full breeches were worn to just
about the knee or shorter, with a fringe
of ribbon loops, and a row or several rows
of the same were arranged at the waist.
A short petticoat just showed the under
breeches, many of which were turned into
a doublet shape by an additional piece
looped up loosely from the knee with a
silk filling; the ribbon loops at the waist
were repeated up the sides of the petticoat.
Silk garters were worn with bows on both
sides of the leg, or a deep lace fall came
from the end of the breeches to the middle
of the calf; a lace setting also filled the
wide top of the boots, which was worn
very low, even to the ankles. These short

176

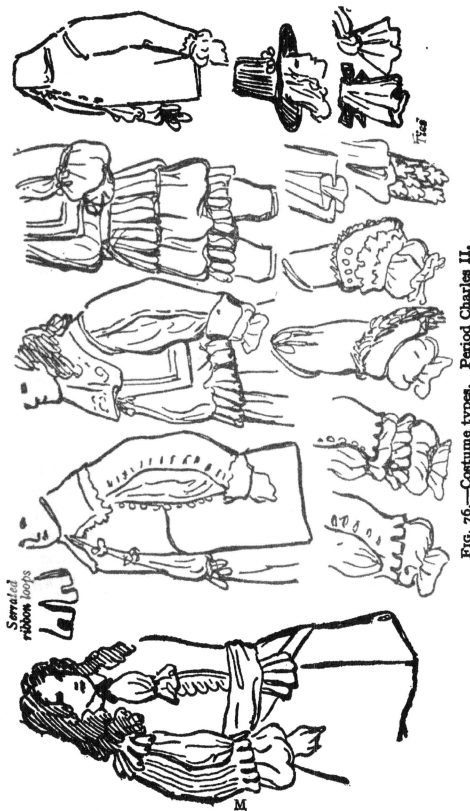

Serrated
ribbon loops

M

Fig.

Fig. 76.—Costume types. Period Charles II.

bell-topped boots were favoured, with high heels and very square toes. Shoes were long and square (or duck-billed) at the toes; and had a high narrow front to the instep, and latchets fastened with a stiffened butterfly bow, besides, at times, a rosette lower down on the front: red heels were in evidence. The sword-band was very wide, and many were decorated with gold embroidery.

SEVENTEENTH CENTURY. JAMES II.
FEMALE.

The hair was still worn full at the sides over a comb, as in the former reign, with curls dropping to the shoulders, but they now began to discard the set-out comb and the little flat curls on the forehead, the hair being of a round shape or parted from the centre and mounted higher and narrower on the head, in the latter part of this reign. The same large hoods and drapes continued in use, and a high goffered head-dress with set-out front began to appear; the same shaped bodice with round low neck showing the shoulders, often set with a stomacher front or jewelled in that form, and smaller decorations of ribbon loops were still favoured. A smaller and

178

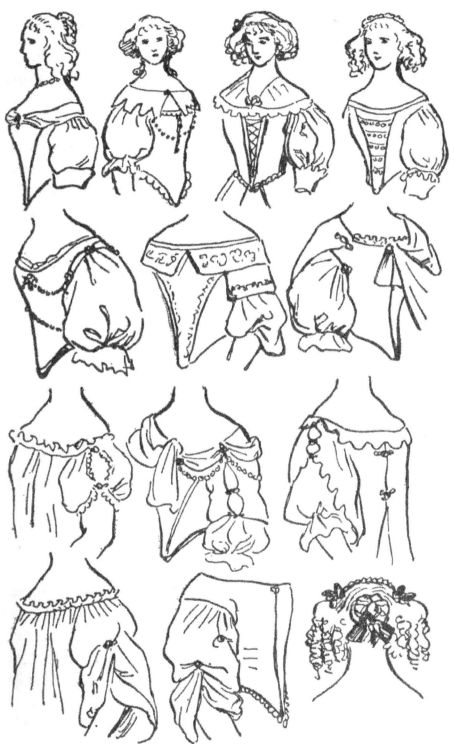

FIG. 77.—Costume notes. Period 1670–1690.

shorter sleeve began to appear with a turned-up cuff, and the gathered-in lawn sleeves and ruffles caught here and there with pearls or clasps as before, besides the same light drapery clasped about the breast front. The overskirt was now looped back, the points being held together, giving a wide display of the underskirt, which was heavily banded or had a jewel setting down the front. Other train skirts, also divided in front, were bordered with drawn silk caught at intervals into long puffs. Very small muffs were the fashion. Shoes increased their pointed shape and rather large heels are to be noted, but some shoes assumed a very narrow square toe; they were either tied from small latchets with a bow, or with buckled latchets. Longer gloves were worn, and large full cloaks with hoods or large drapery wraps when required for outdoor wear.

SEVENTEENTH CENTURY. JAMES II.
MALE.

The same long wig was worn as in the last reign, but the curls were more of a set ringlet type, and embroidered caps were worn when these were taken off. The face was now clean shaven until the 19th

FIG. 78.—Period 1690–1700.

century. Hats also of the older character were retained, but the turned-up three-cornered shape, filled with short feathers, became more settled in fashion, and they were heavily banded with gold braid or lace on the edge.

A smart bow was worn crosswise over the folded lace fall at the neck. The coat was a very long square shape to the knees, the stiff skirt often set out over rather full breeches, which were sometimes " shorts," and just above the knee, the stocking being often brought up above the knee, with a garter just below. The sleeves were short, above or below the elbow, with a turned-up cuff, leaving the full-gathered lawn sleeve with a lace ruffle to show at the wrist. A sash encircled the waist, and often shut in the sword-belt, which hung from the right shoulder. The coat had buttons from the neck to the bottom of the skirt, though the lower buttons were seldom fastened; the sides of the skirt were opened up about 11 inches, and also the back seam to the same height; most seams were heavily decorated with gold, silver braid, or lace, and the pockets were placed rather low down towards the front of the skirt, and were sometimes set vertically.

182

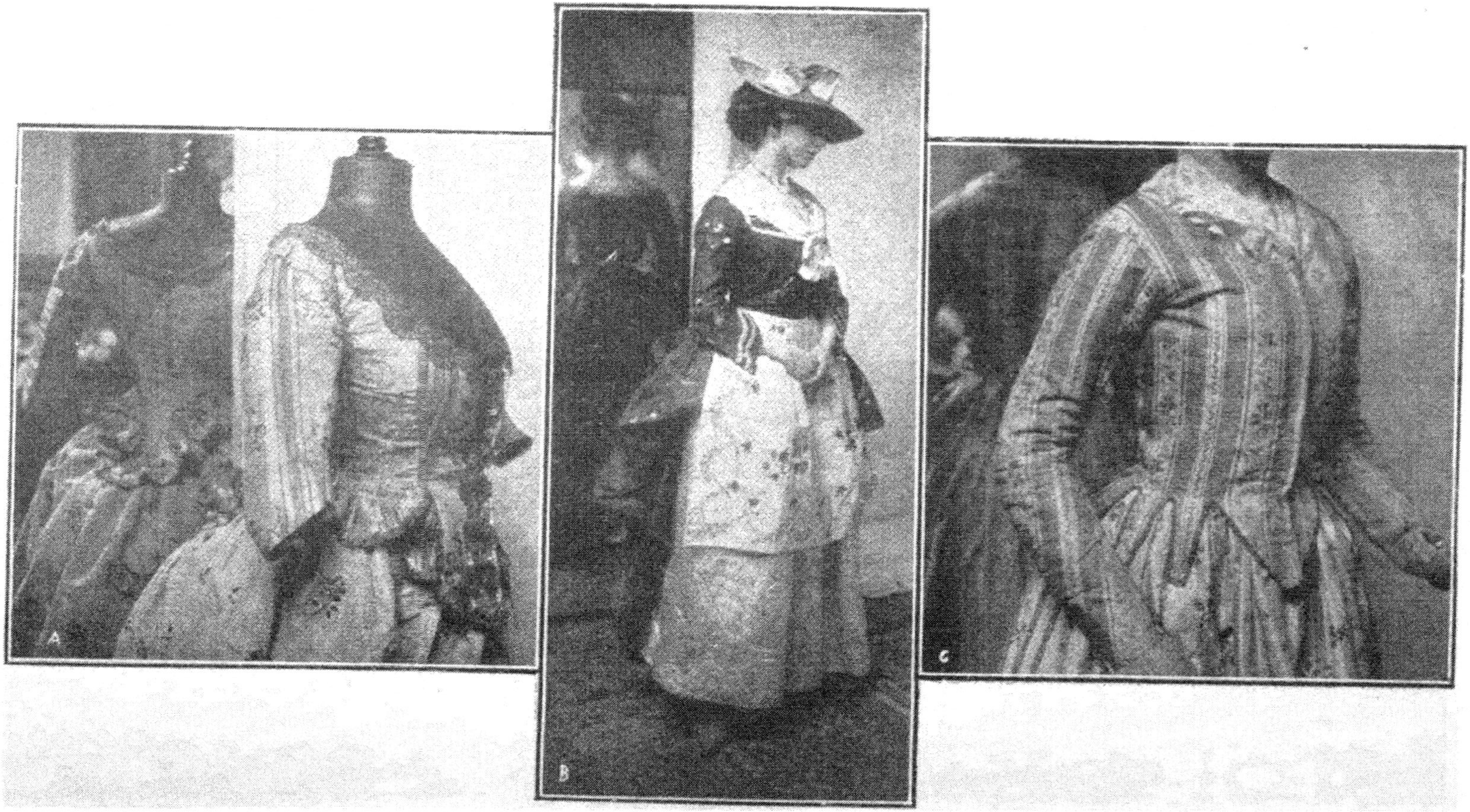

Plate XVIII.—(a) Brocade Bodice. 1770–85.   (b) Flowered Silk Dress. 1750–70.   (c) Silk Brocade Bodice. 1780–95.

FIG. 79.—Period 1688–1702.

Long round capes were still worn, without sleeves, and a collar turned down about 4 inches.

Shoes of a similar shape to those of the later Charles II type were in use, but the heels became larger and the toes not so long; the top of the front was sometimes shaped and turned down. Heavy boots to the knee, with large curved tops, were also in favour, as in the illustration (Fig. 71).

SEVENTEENTH CENTURY. WILLIAM AND MARY. FEMALE.

The hair was now mounted high on top and the front parted with two curls, the rest of the hair being bound on top, or a curl was arranged on either shoulder. A goffered frill head-dress, set on a cap, rose very high, and a long fall of lace, or lappets, came down on either side from the cap, or was gathered in like a small hood at the back. Bare shoulders now began to disappear, the bodice shape coming over the shoulder to a V shape enclosing a stomacher, which was sometimes tabbed or shaped at the point. Many dresses were made in one length, caught together at the waist with a band; the fronts of these skirts were looped back high up, creating a pannier-like fullness at the hips, and narrow hoops came in to set out the skirts, many of which were heavily embroidered with gold. The Watteau-back dress started in this reign; a very early

FIG. 80.—1688–1698.

specimen, at the Victoria and Albert Museum, is most probably of this time (Fig. 85, A). The sleeves worn to the elbow increased in width from the shoulder, and were set with large narrow cuffs gathered with a jewel or bow on the front

185

of the arm. Hoods and cloaks of the same character as described for the last reign continued, and light sticks were carried by the ladies. Very pointed shoes were worn, with large high heels, the top of the front flap in some being shaped into points. Black masks were frequently used, some having long lace falls. Rather small muffs were still the fashion, and beautifully decorated short aprons became a feature with the dress.

SEVENTEENTH CENTURY. WILLIAM AND MARY. MALE.

Wigs of the same long character continued, and were parted in the centre with a raised effect, and variously shaped caps, with turned-up fold or brim, were worn when the wig was taken off.

The beaver or felt hat, turned up three-cornerwise, was now in general use. It is often seen with the brims loose, or sometimes down, especially amongst the lower classes. Both small shapes and large were worn.

Black ties across formal lace cravats, and long lawn cravats, edged with lace, one end of which was sometimes caught

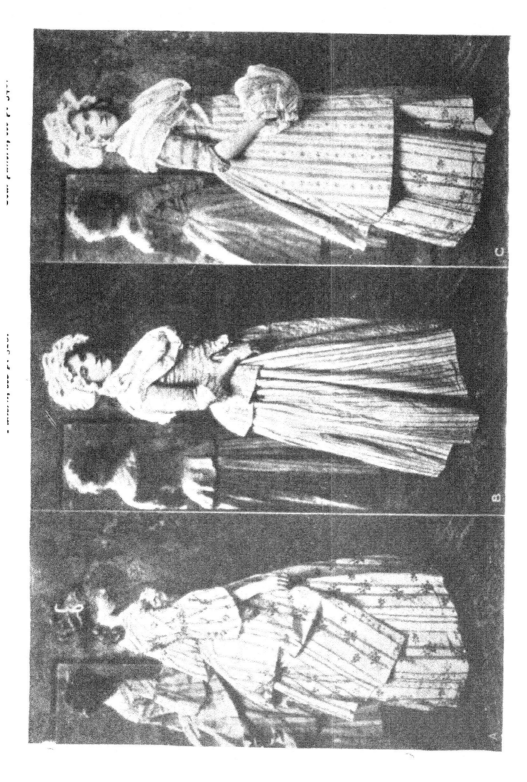

FIG. 81.—Period 1680–1690.

up loosely through the large buttonhole of the coat were worn. Waistcoats were left open well down to the waist; some of these were nearly of the same length as the coat, the skirt being often edged with deep gold fringe.

The coats were of much the same character as in the time of James II, with buttons all down the front, but now it was the mode to button coats just at the waist, allowing the waistcoat to be shown. The sleeves were generally longer, to the middle of the forearm, and the turned-back cuffs became very large and deep, often towards the end of the reign taking a curved shape. The seams, fronts, and pockets were frequently braided as before. A long square waistcoat of rich brocade or embroidered material, about four inches shorter than the coat, was worn; some of these had tight sleeves, which came to the wrist beneath the outer coat-sleeve; otherwise a gathered lawn sleeve with ruffle was worn.

Shoes and boots were practically the same as in the previous reign, with larger high heels and a high square front, with latchets buckled or stiffly tied, and very square toes. Top-boots of the same heavy character continued as in Plate II (see

p. 42). Stockings continued to be worn frequently above the knee outside the breeches, with a garter beneath, and beautifully embroidered clocks to the calf. Muffs were carried by many men, and the gauntlets of gloves had a very angular shape. Patches and make-up were used by the dandies, and the sword was now carried through the side pleats on a waist-belt sometimes worn outside the waistcoat.

CHAPTER VII

THE CHARACTER OF DECORATION AND TRIMMINGS OF THE EIGHTEENTH CENTURY.

The Character of Decoration and Trimmings of the Eighteenth Century

IN the early part to the middle of this century the trimmings were chiefly of gold or silver lace, real lace, and purfled silk, mostly of the same material as the dress: a bow was often worn on the breast, and also in the front of the sleeve cuff. Purfled or ruched trimming generally ran down the front of the dress from the neck to the hem of the skirt in the Second Georgian dress, and gathered borders or decorations of curved forms were in use. The skirts usually had only one flounce till the reign of George III, when the trimmings became more elaborate, and gauze and imitation flowers were festooned upon the skirts, with ribbons and tassels and padded designs standing out in strong relief; some charming gimp trimmings are also seen.

The lace ruffles of a fan shape which finished the earlier sleeves till about 1745 were sometimes of lace, interwoven with gold, silver, and coloured silk needlework, and this was no doubt the forerunner of the use of the more solid material itself. The setting of the sleeve finish is interesting to note all through this period, for it was beautifully treated in balancing the effect of the dress. The square cuff with the deep lace fall was big in style, and the later closely-fitted elbow piece, richly gathered, was happily conceived, but no finer setting could have been applied to the sack-back dress than the large fan or double fan with its lace fall. The edges of the early fan-finished sleeves were of curved and scalloped forms, the latter shaping often being seen in the later sleeves.

With George III we notice designs in straw work, decorations of imitation flowers in ribbon-work and various materials, and much taste in the choice of colour schemes, while the tassels of this period were delightful creations. The designs of stuffs at the early part of the

The Charac-
ter of
Decoration
and
Trimmings
of the
Eighteenth
Century
century were generally of fine strong colour blends, but in the middle period there was much questionable taste displayed in the heavy massing of patterns, but this soon improved with the striped character crossed by running flowers which was quite ideal in type for costume keeping, grace, and lightness, with a beautiful interchange of colour.

The quilted silk and satin petticoats are a special feature to note in these times; many simple and effective designs were in use, and they added much glitter to the scheme. Aprons were also beautiful examples of needlework, and were worn with the best of dresses to the middle of the century; the earlier ones generally had a scalloped edging, and many had pockets; gold lace edging or fringe was often used in the time of George II, and they were all finely decorated with needlework in gold, silver, or coloured silks. The white aprons were also of consummate needlecraft, and hanging pockets worn at the sides were also a decorated feature, but these only showed when the dress was worn tucked up. The later style of dress became much simpler, consisting chiefly of gathered flounce settings, fichus, and large mob caps; these were often daintily em- broidered with tambour work and large bow and sash settings, making delightful costumes.

Bags, muffs, gloves, and shoes were all chosen for the display of needlecraft, while artists and jewellers used all their skill on the fans, patch-boxes, and étuis, and even the dress materials were often painted by hand, while many painted Chinese silks were also utilised.

EIGHTEENTH CENTURY. ANNE. FEMALE.

The hair was dressed in a simple manner, with two curls parted from the centre of the forehead, and curved inwards on the brow. A loose ringlet or two were brought on to the left shoulder, the rest being gathered into a back-knot. Feathers or flowers were arranged on top, generally with a pair of lace lappets falling to the back; these also adorned the cap, which still bore the front goffered frills set out as in the last reign, but these were diminished in size and were mostly of one row. We note probably the last stage of this style appearing in a print of Hogarth's, dated 1740.

FIG. 82.—Bodice types. Period 1690–1720.

FIG. 83.—Costume type.   1695-1710.

Hoods and capes or cloaks, and long black fichus or wraps, were the chief coverings, as the head-dress did not allow of hats being worn, but with the small frilled caps a little straw hat, or a low-crowned felt with a largish brim, are seen, and a small lace frill round the neck began to appear. Bodices with a low curved neck often had a short skirt or shaped pieces, as well as a shaped short sleeve over a gathered lawn one, while many wore long sleeves to the wrist, and a waistbelt is sometimes noted. There was also the sleeve spreading in width to the elbow, with a turned-up square cuff. The front of the bodice may be remarked with bands fastening across, and this became a feature in many dresses later in this century, otherwise it set closely over the shoulders to a V shape at the waist, and was filled with a stomacher of fine needlework, bows, or the ends of the lawn fichu laced or caught in by a big bow. A full, loose gown, with the fullness pleated to back and front, came in, the front being held by a bow and the back allowed to fall loose or crossed with a large bow at the back of waist, as in the museum specimen, Fig. 85. This became the more elaborate sack-back dress.

196

FIG. 84.—Period 1700–1725.

The skirts began to be set out in a bell form, and trains were in much favour; the overskirts were parted in front, and many looped up to the back in a similar manner to the last reign. Small aprons of fine embroidery were worn with the best of dresses, and embroidered pockets are seen when the skirts were thrown back. Petticoats of fine quilting became much appreciated, and tall sticks were carried by ladies. Pointed shoes with high heels and latchets tied or buckled, the top of the fronts being mostly cut into four points, or they had a square finish.

EIGHTEENTH CENTURY. ANNE. MALE.

The wigs of the full ringlet style were still the fashion, but a simpler character is noticeable, the hair being combed back off the forehead and allowed to fall in looser waves. But many began to set a mode of smaller "coiffure," with their own hair caught in curls by a bow at the back, and curls over each ear. Powder came into use with the smart set, and a big bow and bag to finish the back of wig appeared, giving a smarter appearance to the white hair.

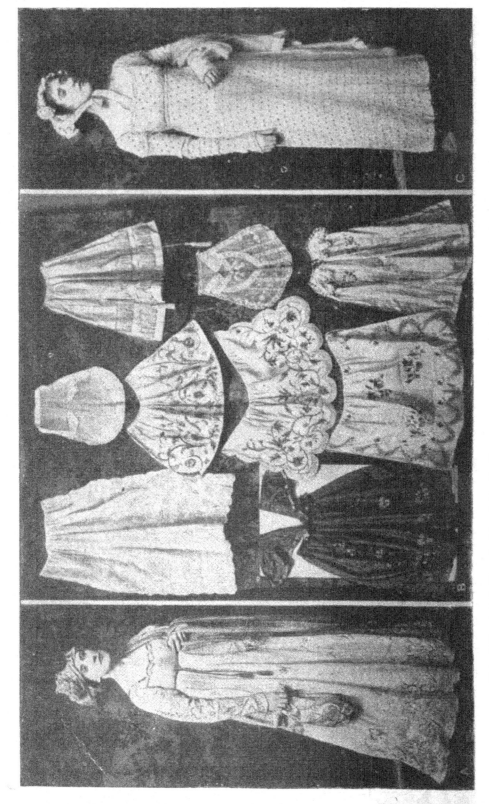

Plate XX.—(a) Gold-embroidered Muslin Dress. 1795–1805.   (b) Nine Aprons.   Between 1690 and 1850.
(c) Dress of Spotted Stockinette.   1795–1808.

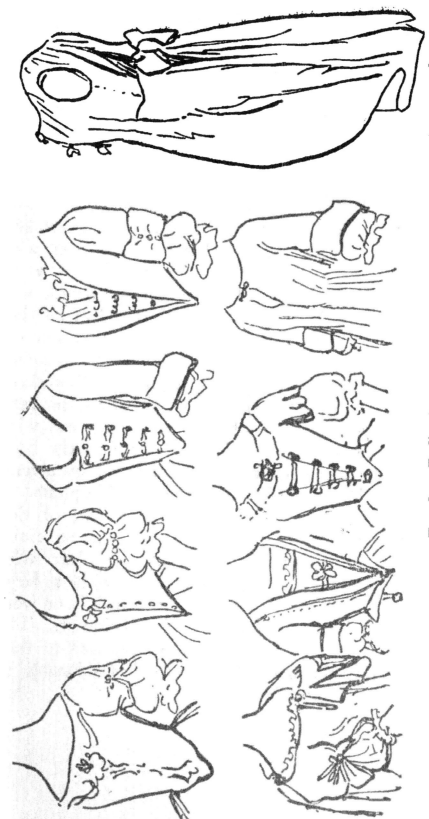

FIG. 85.—Bodice types, 1700–1725.

The hat, sometimes of white felt, was the same three-cornered type, edged with feathers and banded with broad gold braids or silver lace. The neckwear was a bind of lawn, with a long fall finished with lace.

The coat remained long to the knees, but took a greater fullness in the side pleats of the skirt. Large buttons and buttonholes, 3 inches long, are seen, with the same on the cuff, which was worn very large, often 9 inches broad, and mostly of a curved outline, and of another coloured brocade; a tight undersleeve is also seen with these. The coat was sometimes heavily decorated with needlework or braids of gold down the front, pockets, seams, and cuffs. The pocket was wide and set higher in the skirt, and the back opening of coat was decorated by several horizontal braids to the two side pleats.

A long, full-skirted waistcoat, of rich materials or needlework, was at times braided and fringed at the skirt with gold, the pockets covered with a large flap, and five buttons fastened it or were placed as decorations just below it. The front buttons were often reduced to four at the waist, as it was still fashionable to show the lawn shirt.

200

Breeches were of the same cut as in the former reign, with five or six side buttons at the knee, and stockings with embroidered clocks were worn rolled over outside the breeches as before.

Shoes were square at the toes and not quite so long, while the heels were still rather heavy, and red was the mode. They had a high square top at the front instep, and buckles fastened the latchets. Muffs were often carried by the dandies, and walking-sticks, with tassel and loop, were slung on the arm; besides a sword, which, passing through the side pleats and out at the back, helped to set out the coat, which was often stiffened in the skirts. Gloves, with short gauntlets very angular or curved in shape, were trimmed with gold fringe; the backs were also richly embroidered with gold or silver.

EIGHTEENTH CENTURY. GEORGE I.
FEMALE.

The hair was very simply gathered from the forehead and taken up to a knot of curls at the back. Occasionally a group of curls was allowed to fall behind, or a curl was arranged to fall on one shoulder,

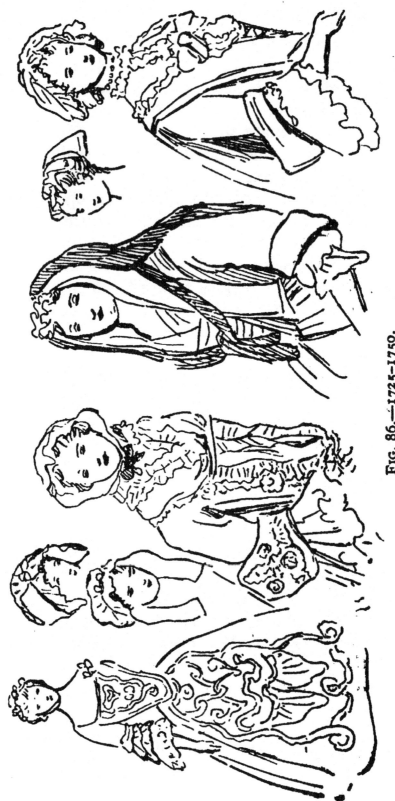

FIG. 86.—1725-1750.

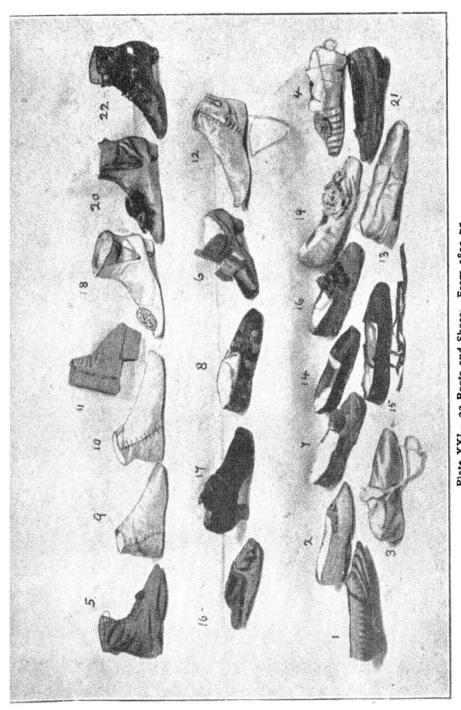

Plate XXI.—23 Boots and Shoes. From 1800-75.

1. 1800-1820.	9. 1820-1830.	7. 1850-1865.	21. 1860-1875.
2. ,,	10. ,,	14 & 15. ,,	11. ,,
3. 1810-1828.	13. 1830-1855.	4. ,,	18. ,,
5. 1820-1830.	16. ,,	6. ,,	20. ,,
8. ,,	16A. ,,	17. ,,	19. ,,
		12	22

FIG. 87.—Period 1725–1750.

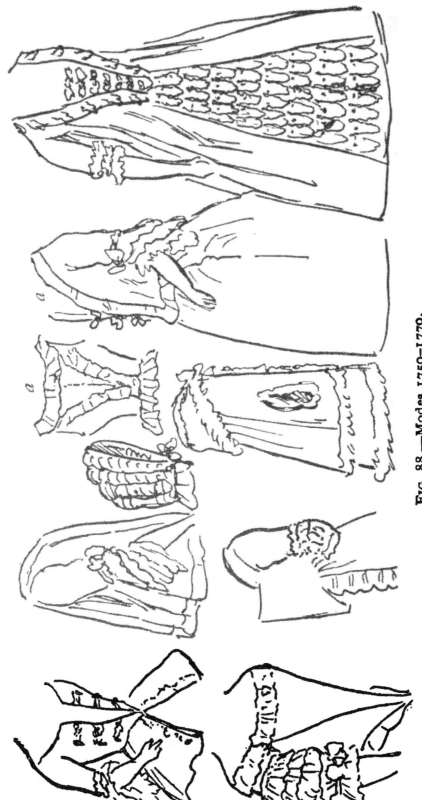

FIG. 88.—Modes, 1750–1770.

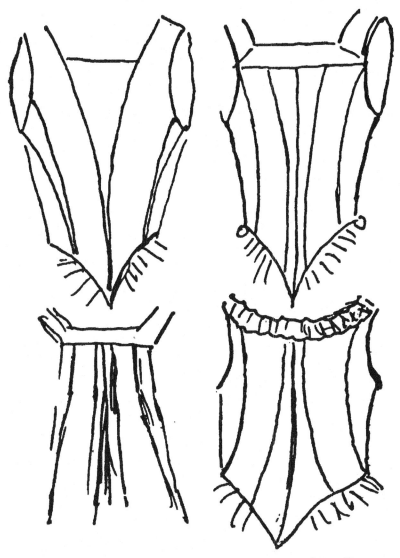

FIG. 89.—Various Styles in Cut Back of Bodice.

and waved curls of the Queen Anne type were still seen on many people. Caps, with long dropping points in front, sometimes tied under the chin or with long lappets at the back, were the chief favourites, also a small frilled cap. Shallow-crowned straw hats with various widths of brim; hoods and capes, both short and long, are seen, besides light silks draped from the hair to the waist, feathers, flowers, and ribbons being worn in the head-dress. Richly embroidered aprons were worn with the finest dresses.

The sack-back dress was very full, and started right across the shoulders in two double box-pleats, which were kept trim by being sewn flat for two to four inches down. Sleeves to the elbow were rather full, and gathered at the shoulders, with a square cuff often decorated with a bow in front, and a fan of lace, sometimes in several rows, fell from beneath. Sleeves finishing in a shaped edge are occasionally seen. The skirts were made for the very round hoop setting, and were gathered in flat pleats on either hip. A wide pleat or two came from the shoulders down the front sometimes as a continuation of the sack-back. These pleats, meeting at the waist,

206

formed a V shape, which was filled by an embroidered stomacher, or made of the same material, crossed by bands, bows, or rows of lace. The flat front pleat was occasionally embroidered, and gradually widened to the bottom of the skirt. Very pointed toes to the shoes, and high heels, with tied or buckled latchets, are seen, the tops of the front often being shaped into four points.

EIGHTEENTH CENTURY. GEORGE I.
MALE.

Long, full wigs are still seen amongst older men, but several new shapes appear as illustrated (Fig. 90), and the black bow and bag became very large; a black ribbon attached to it, with a bow in front, came round the neck. We also see the ends of the wig made into a long, tight pigtail. Hats were of the same three-cornered shape, rather fuller in size, and the feathered edging was still favoured. A hat of the type of Fig. 105 was also worn; and the loose cap with a tassel was put on when the wig was removed (see Fig. 104).

The neck had the same lawn bind with a long lace ruffle, and the coat the same

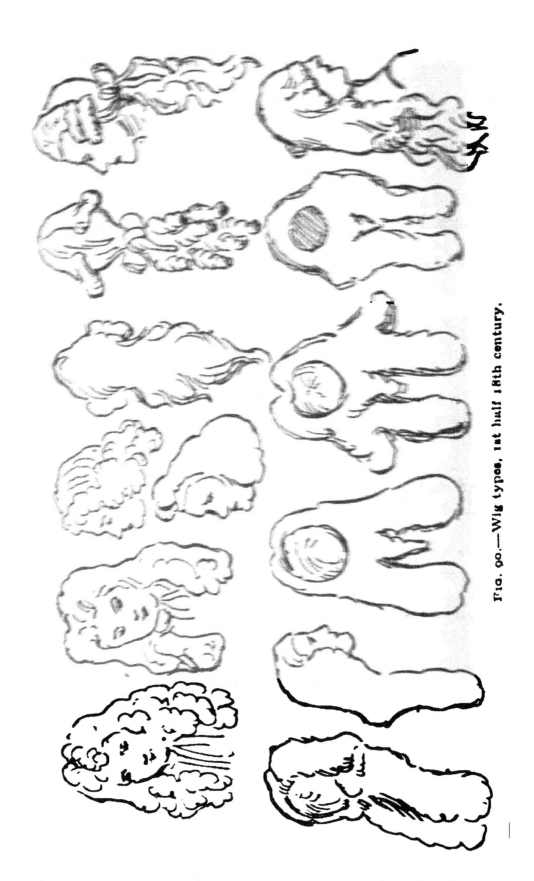

Fig. 90.—Wig types, 1st half 18th century.

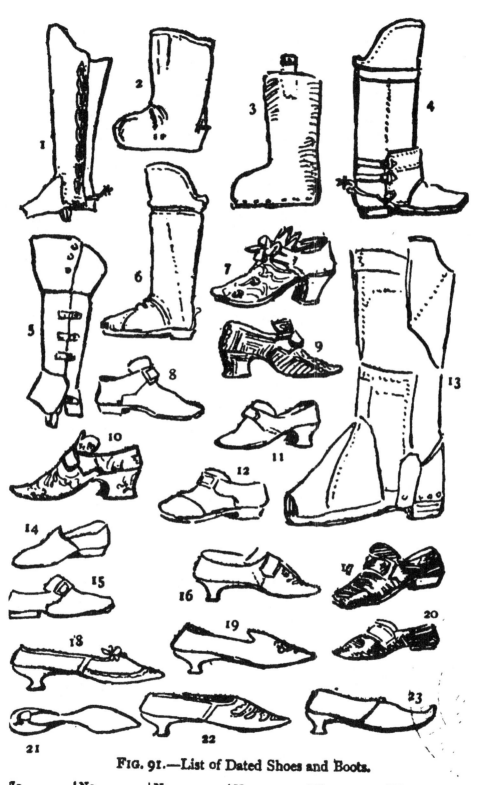

FIG. 91.—List of Dated Shoes and Boots.

No.	No.	No.	No.	No.	No.
1. 1700–1750.	5. 1700–1760.	9. 1700–1740.	13. 1760–1800.	17. 1740–1780.	21. Sole of shoe
2. 1700–1780.	6. 1720–1780.	10. 1740–1760.	14. 1730–1760.	18. 1786–1796.	No. 22.
3. 1700–1780.	7. 1690–1720.	11. 1702–1720.	15. 1740–1770.	19. 1774–1784.	22. 1776–1800.
4. 1700–1750.	8. 1700–1750.	12. 1730–1750.	16. 1770–1780.	20. 1775–1790.	23. 1780–1790.

full cut as in the last reign, and the large
rounded cuff was still in favour, but many
varieties of size were now worn. A vertical
pocket is seen occasionally on cloth coats,
also a cape and turned-down collar are
noted, while several appear with a very
small upright collar. Buttons were still
worn on some coats, right down the front;
but on many coats the buttons stopped
level with the pocket.

A short-skirted coat came in amongst
the dandies towards the end of the reign,
and was stiffened out on the skirts; these
mostly had a tighter sleeve and cuff. The
same decorations continued in use. Waistcoats were much the same, and were cut
to the length of the coats, or about four
inches shorter; they were buttoned higher,
the lace often falling outside.

Breeches were the same in cut, fastened
with six buttons and a buckle at the side
of the knee. The stockings, usually decorated with clocks, were still worn rolled
outside the knee amongst smart people.
The stiff high boots or gaiters generally
had a full curved piece at the top, and
short gaiters to the calf are also to be
noticed.

The shoes were square-toed or of a

roundish form, with a short or rather high square front, and heels of various heights. Patches and make-up were used by the fops, and swords and sticks carried, the latter being very high, to 46 inches.

EIGHTEENTH CENTURY. GEORGE II. FEMALE.

The hair was treated in much the same manner as with George I up to the end of this reign—gathered back from the forehead to a bunch of curls at the back. The small hats and caps, often worn together, continued of the same character; the dresses also remained similar in cut. The sack-back dress was supreme in the fifties, when it was set with panniers, together with the hoops, but the latter were not so much worn towards the end of this reign, except for the "grand dress." Quilted petticoats were much worn, but flounces are not a feature on the skirts till the latter part of this period. The simpler dress was of various lengths, and was at times worn quite short up to 1740. The corset bodice was still in use, with lawn sleeves: square cuffs and lace ruffles held the lead throughout this time, but the fan-

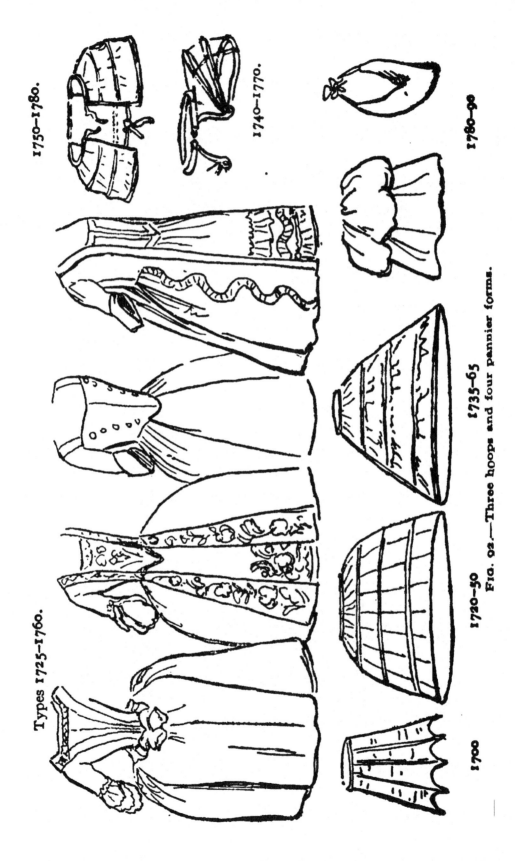

1750–1780.

1740–1770.

1780–90.

1735–65.

Types 1725–1760.

1720–50.

1700

Fig. 92.—Three hoops and four pannier forms.

Quilted designs on Petticoats, 18th century

FIG. 93.

shaped sleeve finish to the elbow, in the same material as the dress, began to appear about 1750, generally with a waved or scalloped edge. Pointed toes and high-heeled shoes continued, with either tied or buckled latchets, and long gloves and mittens were in use.

EIGHTEENTH CENTURY. GEORGE II.
MALE.

Wigs with double points at the back, short curled or of long pigtailed shapes, some with side curls, others curled all round the front, were worn. Large bows and bags, or no bows, finished the back hair, and the bow to the front of the neck was in use from the early part of this reign. Long coats, as in the last reign, and short coats with stiffened skirts were used; many with braided seams and fronts, also a braided opening at the back. Large round cuffs and big square ones, caped coats, and coats with turn-down collars were all in the mode, and the "maccaroni" fashions started about 1760, with absurdities in small hats, clubbed wigs, and very short coats. High sticks and crook sticks, canes and swords continued in use.

The pocket flaps were of a curved form,

214

Pattern of Bodice, see p. 316.

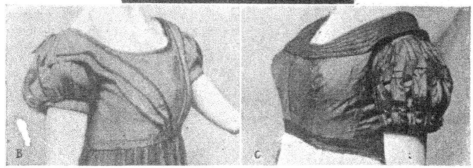

Plate XXII.—(a) Linen Dress. 1795–1808.
(b) Silk Bodice. 1825–30.
(c) Silk Bodice. 1818–25.

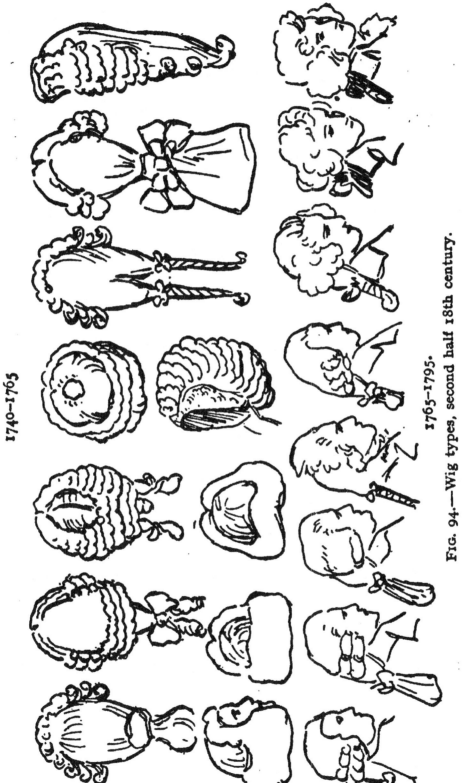

1740–1765

1765–1795.

FIG. 94.—Wig types, second half 18th century.

with a rounded centre still, and many of the shoes had a high square front, high heels, and square toes: according to the caricature prints of Boitard, the fashionable hats were smaller in 1730, and much

FIG. 95.—First Half Eighteenth Century.

larger ten years later; very full skirts at the former date, and smaller and less stiffened at the latter. Stockings were often still worn outside the knee. Shoes reached an extreme high square front at the latter date, and gloves with curved or square cuffs are to be noted.

This long reign, like that of Queen Victoria, embraces several changes of style. Up till about 1785 white powder was still used for the hair, reaching its fullest extravagance in the middle of the seventies, set with pearls, bandeaus, caps, lace, flowers and feathers, and about 1776 the top was widened considerably. The front hair, gathered from the forehead, was pressed in a forward curve over a high pad, with one to three curls at the sides and one at the shoulders, the back hair being arranged in a loose loop, curled on the top and set with a large bow at the back; a small round hat with very small low crown (usually decorated with flowers and silks gathered into puffs, or ribbons and small feathers) was tilted right on the front. About 1780 large mob caps with a big bow on the front came in, and were generally worn together with the tall-crowned hat or the large-brimmed hat in favour at this time. A cape with smallish hood worn in the earlier reigns was supplanted about 1777 by the calash, a huge

217

1795

FIG. 96.—Costume notes, 1770–1780.

FIG. 99.—Hats during period 1790–1800.

hood set out with whalebone which came
to cover the full head-dresses. The heavier
caped or hooded cloak, sometimes with
side opening for the arms, and usually
trimmed with fur, still remained in use to
1800.

The bodice retained the same shape as
in the former reign, rather longer in the
points back and front, with a large fan
finish to the sleeve, double or single; this
became supplanted by a much-gathered
elbow-piece, sometimes eight inches deep,
gathered in four rows. Small drawn
gathers started round the waist of the
skirt, for the side panniers and hoops were
being less worn, except for the "smart
gown," but bunching, reefing, and looping took their place in effect, and quilted
petticoats remained while this character of
dress lasted. The later sack-back dress
was sewn tighter to the body, and
usually started in a narrower set at the
back, while the full pleat from the shoulder
down the front went out, and the neck
was more displayed by lower bodice fronts,
which continued to be set with bows,
jewels, lace, or embroidery. Sack-back
jackets were often worn in the seventies;
when the sack began to disappear, it took

222

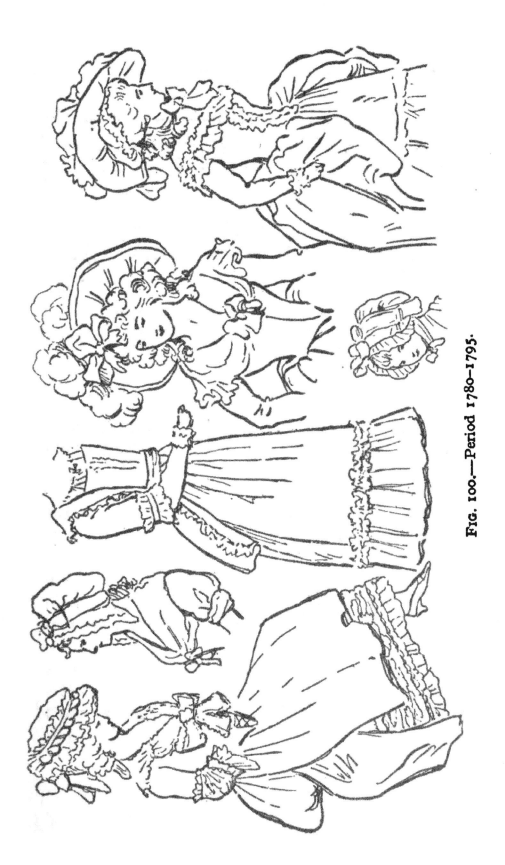

FIG. 100.—Period 1780–1795.

the form of overlapped seams on the bodice. The decorated side pockets are noted in prints showing tuck-up dresses to 1775. The jacket bodice of the same form described in the preceding reign was perhaps more in evidence till 1780, not so long in the skirt as in the earlier reigns, but after this date it took a longer skirt, which was often pleated at the back, with a very low neck and short waist.

About 1780 we find a change of style appearing in a shorter waist, with less pointed setting, having often a rounded point or square tabs, and even a shaped finish to the corset front, which was sometimes used like a waistcoat effect under the cut-away dresses seen after 1770 (see Fig. 99, p. 221). A general tendency to imitate male attire is apparent, and the front of the bodice was set with lapels and straps buttoned across (though I have noted this latter character in the early part of this century), and long coats with this character were much worn, with two or three capes. The sleeves are sometimes set over a tight undersleeve, in fact the longer sleeve to the wrist became fashionable. With this change a short gathered skirt is seen on some bodices, and

224

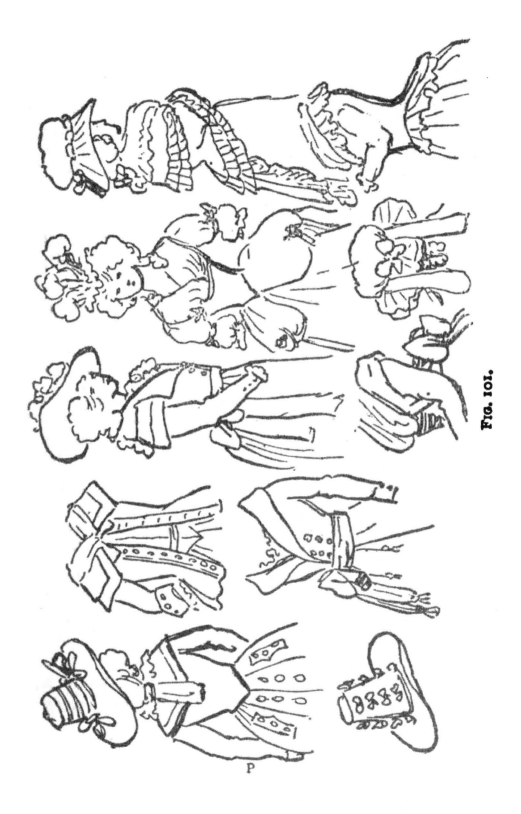

FIG. 101.

the full gathered skirt was bunched out at the back on a bustle, of which I give an illustration (p. 212), the low neck being filled with a large lawn fichu; a wide belt was generally worn, or a wide sash and bow at the back or side is seen with the lighter dresses, these being simple in style, just gathered at the waist, with short full sleeves set with a frill, and another frill was also arranged round the neck.

About 1790 the mode again began to change to a classic style, still higher in the waist, with a short tight sleeve, at times puffed in the upper part, or an outer and under sleeve, as per illustration A, Plate XXII (see p. 215). The fronts of this type of bodice were mostly buttoned or pinned up to the shoulders over a tight underfront, the skirt opening about 18 inches at the sides, thus saving a fastening at the back. I have illustrated some very interestingly cut jackets of this period from my collection, as A, Plate XXIV (see p. 231); the sleeves were very long and were ruckled on the arm, as likewise were the long gloves or mittens of this time. A long scarf or drape was carried with this style, and a round helmet-like hat in straw or a turban was adopted. High sticks were

226

FIG. 102.—Period 1790–1800.

FIG. 103.—Costume notes, 1790–1800.

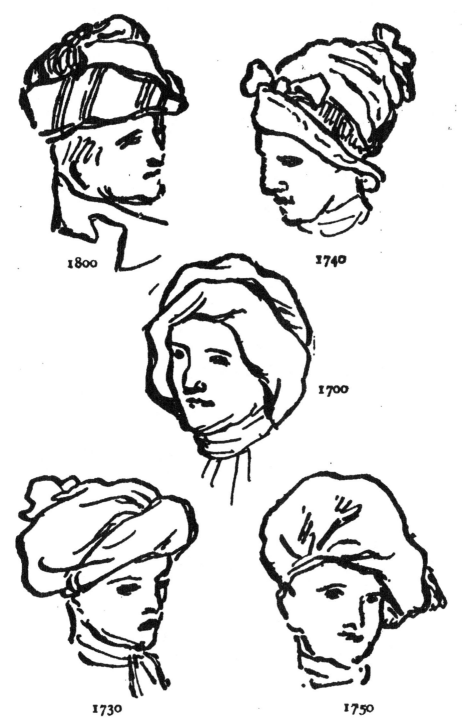

1800

1740

1700

1730

1750

FIG. 104.—Lounge Caps worn during removal of Wig.

still carried by ladies till the nineties, and umbrellas or parasols; the former came into vogue about 1770, the latter about six years later. Muffs of beautifully embroidered silk and satin were set with purfled trimmings, gold and silver lace, or bows and ribbons; otherwise they were of furs or feathers. They remained rather small up to 1780, when a very large shape set in, which continued till the end of the reign; the quantity of beautiful fans of this century must be so well known as to need no description. The highest artistry was concentrated on them.

Shoes at the beginning of this reign were set on very high spindle heels; the toe-front became rounded, the instep-front a pointed shape, and wide latchets were buckled till about 1785, but fashion discarded them earlier; for about 1780 the shoes became very small at the heel, and pointed again at the toe. When the latchets went out, the pointed instep remained for a time, but a low round front appeared, and the heel practically vanished just before 1800. These later shoes were decorated on the front by needlework or incised leather openwork underlaid with another colour. The soles at this time

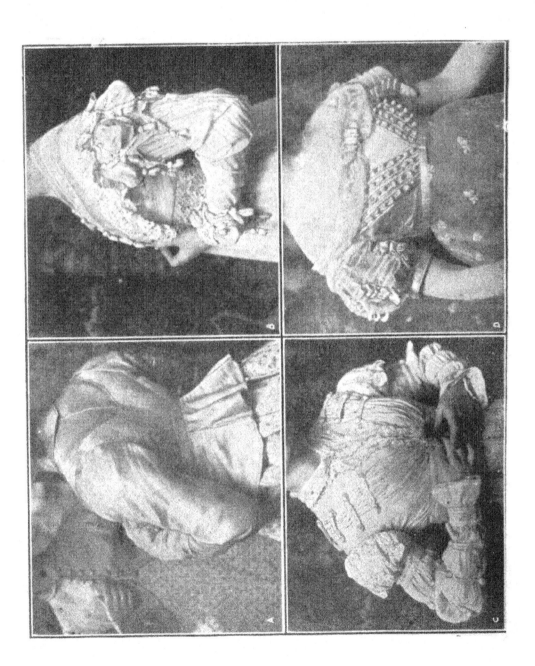

were extremely quaint in shape, and the shoes were tied sandal fashion up the ankle.

EIGHTEENTH CENTURY. GEORGE III TO 1800. MALE.

The wigs, which were rather high in the front of the crown in the earlier part, began to cast off the most eccentric forms, and became just curled, rather full at the sides, and tied with a bow at the back: dull pink powder became a favoured hue from about 1780; most people began to return to their own hair, and one might see many without long hair in the nineties. The last type of dressing the hair in imitation of the wig form was a long, tightly braided pigtail at the back, with one or even two side curls over the ear, and side whiskers were allowed to fill up to them; thus when the short hair set the fashion, side whiskers came in.

Hats were still worn of the three-cornered shape, but the favourites became a front cockade hat and a hat with a rounded crown and rather wide brim, sometimes turned up on one side; a short type of top-hat was also often seen, and later became the fashion. The same lawn and lace cravat developed into more of a plain white stock, with a frilled shirt-front.

The coat was worn much tighter in the arms and was smartly cut, with the fronts running away into a narrow tailed skirt. The pockets often began to take a plain square form, with or without buttons; the buttons on the front of the coat stopped at the waist—many cuffs are seen without them; and the side pleats, set more to the back, were pressed and narrower. Both the plain and turn-over collars were set up high in the neck, large cut-steel buttons were introduced in the early seventies, and many fancy china buttons, besides the gilt silver and paste ones were in use. A new type of coat made its appearance with a high turn-over collar and large lapels, and a sudden cut-in of the coat-front high in the waist, giving a very long-tailed effect to the skirt. A cuff shape with these was mostly made in one with the sleeve and buttoned at the side towards the back, and when the cuff was additional, it seldom had buttons, as formerly.

A greatcoat with one, two, or three capes was a picturesque garment, and a leather-covered bottle was often carried

232

FIG. 105.

when riding a distance, of which I have an example in my collection.

Waistcoats, which had become much shorter, were now giving place to a type with a straight-across front and turned-back lapels at the neck; these large lapels were mostly worn outside over the coat lapel. The waistcoats were often double-breasted with an embroidered design down the front between the double row of buttons, and the straight pockets of these had no flaps; they shortened at the waist in character with the lapelled coat, but were worn lower than the cut-in shape of the coat, showing about 3 inches when the coat was fastened. Breeches became very tight, and trousers begin to appear after 1790. Striped stockings and suits were much in favour. Top-boots with rather long brown tops were worn, or high boots with a curved top, with a gold tassel set in front, were seen. The shoes with latchets and buckles had a low front on the instep, and from about 1780 took a rather pointed oval toe shape; the heels were mostly worn shorter. Swords were not so much in use except on great occasions, but sword-sticks were carried, and heavy club-sticks were fashionable before 1800. Patches were little

Plate XXV.—(*a*) Silk Dress. 1800–10.
(*b*) Cotton Dress. 1800–10.
(*c*) Embroidered Muslin Dress. 1820–30 (*Pattern, see p.* 339).
(*d*) Silk Gauze Dress. 1824–30.

Facing page 234.

1745 1777

1785 1795

FIG. 106.

used after the seventies, but the snuff-box was still indispensable. The double long purse with central rings and tassels at the ends was carried, of knitted silk or of leather, the former with steel beads and coloured silks worked together after 1780: small bag purses were also in use, usually set in gilt mounts and made in the same methods with a tassel below.

CHAPTER VIII

CHARACTER OF TRIMMINGS OF THE NINETEENTH CENTURY.

DURING the later part of the 18th century, a great deal of tinsel drawn work was done on fine muslin, and became beautifully treated in delicate design on the hem and down the front of many of the high-waisted dresses as in Fig. A, Plate XXIII (see p. 218). Later on towards the twenties we see a great deal of effective coarse work in heavy gold tinsel, and at the same time to the forties a number of dresses were ably enriched with fine gold thread.

The white embroidery in the earlier trimmings of this period, of which I give examples in Plate XXIV (see p. 231), was remarkable for its wealth of fancy; the chief beauty of these dresses was the delightful treatment of gathered effects, and with the

237

reign of George IV we note the gradual return of the longer pointed bodice, with the growth of very full sleeves, also the increase in the size and fuller set-out of the skirts over the stiff flounced drill petticoats. The V-shaped Bertha setting to neck and shoulders began to establish itself, and became a great feature through the thirties and forties; the first signs of it appear about 1814. Varieties of materials were used to great advantage in designing, and drawn tulle trimmings were happily introduced to soften hard shapes and colours. The shoulder fullness also began to be neatly drawn in and held by straps, which gave a charming character to many bodices.

From 1816 choice work in piped shapes, often of flower forms decorated with pearls or beads, was set on fine net, as seen in Plates XXIII and XXIX (see pp. 218, 263). The attraction to the thirties was the happy effects gained by the bow and flower looping on the flounces, and these ripened in fancy and variety through the forties. Braiding was adopted in the thirties with a rather charming treatment of tassels down the front of the dress; the polonaises of this time were

238

also effective and simple, caught here and there with posies of flowers, and we find this fashion again revived in the sixties.

With the reign of George IV we notice an increasing choice of strong coloured effects, which culminated in the mid-Victorian era in raw colour and violent shot silks, velvets, and heavy fringes, but one may see that many of these dresses of bright pure tone looked exceedingly refined and were quite stately. A remarkable dress is Fig. A, Plate XXXII (see p. 279), which is of very strong bright blue; its only enrichment being a curved line of folded silk. All these dresses from 1800 were delightfully embellished with embroidered fichus, light scarves of frail gauze, crêpe, or Norwich silk, and in the Victorian times capes and V-shaped shawls; fascinating lace ruffles and tuck-in fronts to the bodice necks, of frills and bands of embroidery, broke the severity or bareness of many dresses. An endless variety of fascinating caps and lace head-lappets was pinned or caught into the hair at the wearer's fancy; besides the bows, flowers, and jewels (especially pearls) which have always played an important part in the coiffure from early times, the chatelaines and bags, fobs, fans, and lace or silk hand-kerchiefs all give the artist a note of extra colour when desired. The cruel period of taste really came with the seventies, though one can trace many quaint and interesting cuts in the bodices and skirts of this time; but the "grand dress" of complicated drapings, heavily fringed or braided, was a "set piece" which, let us hope, will never appear again.

The long stocking-purse which began to appear in the late 17th century was up to 1820 sometimes carried tucked through the belt; it was set with a pair of metal rings and tassels of steel or gilt beads. Small and large circular and bag-shaped purses were also in use; all these were made in coloured silk threads enriched with steel, gilt, or coloured beads, the latter shapes being set in chased metal mounts, the circular ones generally having a fringe and the bag shape a small tassel or heavy drop. These shapes can also be seen in coloured leathers with a leather tassel, besides the plain money-bag with a draw-string.

The hair up to 1808 was gathered into a knot of curls at the back of the head, rather high up, with a small curl at the sides in front of the ear. Later the knot was set more on the top, and the side curls were made more of a feature, several being arranged at the sides. Numerous varieties of large and small brimmed hats, bonnets, and turbans are seen, and several masculine top-hats and cockade hats may be noted late in this reign. The usual feather decorations and large ribbons or flowers were in use, and a handkerchief was sometimes bound over the top of the straw hat and tied under the chin.

The classic high-waisted dress continued till 1808, and was often beautifully decorated with white embroidery and gold or tinsel, as in A, Plates XX and XXIII (see pp. 199, 218), and the frontispiece is a lovely white example. There were several interesting drapings, one being a cord hanging from the back of the shoulder to loop up the train of the dress, as in A, Plate XXII (see p. 215). The simple tunic shapes are better described

FIG. 107.—Costume notes, 1811-1812.

FIG. 108.—Costume notes, 1814–1816.

by the illustrations: more originality was essayed in design after the last-mentioned date. A high Vandyked lace collar and fan setting to the shoulders appeared, and many interesting dresses of a plain cut, mostly in velvet and silks, were worn about 1810–12. A gathered sleeve drawn tight at intervals was often seen up to 1816, when embroidered ruffles and frills decorated most of the necks and skirts, and a braided type of character, rather military in effect with beautifully piped edgings, came in from about 1817. Spencer bodices were an additional interest at this period, and a short puff sleeve was generally banded or caught with bows; these being often worn over a fairly loose long sleeve gathered by a wristband. Dresses were worn shorter from about 1810. Charming lace and embroidered fichus crossed the shoulders, and long scarf-capes were thrown round the neck and were often tied round behind, as in the 18th century; long capes with points and tassels in front fell to the knees, and a simple pelisse with cape became a pleasing feature. Bags were always carried, of which there is a variety of shapes in the plates; long gloves or mittens were generally worn. Parasols of a flat shape, or others

1818

1815

1816

1816

Muff

1818

1816

1819

FIG. 109.

with round or pagoda shaped tops are seen, many being edged with a deep fringe. Long purses were often tucked through the waistband.

The pointed shoe, tied sandal fashion up the leg, and with no heel, remained through this reign, but a round-toed low shoe, tied on in the same manner, began to supersede it about 1810.

NINETEENTH CENTURY. GEORGE III.
MALE.

Wigs had practically gone out, except for a few of the latter type of the 18th century amongst elderly people. The hair was now worn short, and left rather full on the front, with short side-whiskers. Plain black or white stocks tied with a front bow, and a starched or unstarched collar with a frilled or gathered shirt-front were in use. A tie-pin or stud was also seen in the centre of the stock or frilling.

The same hats as in the latter part of the 18th century continued for a time, but the top-hat had established its favour, and assumed various shapes throughout this reign.

The coats were set with very high turn-

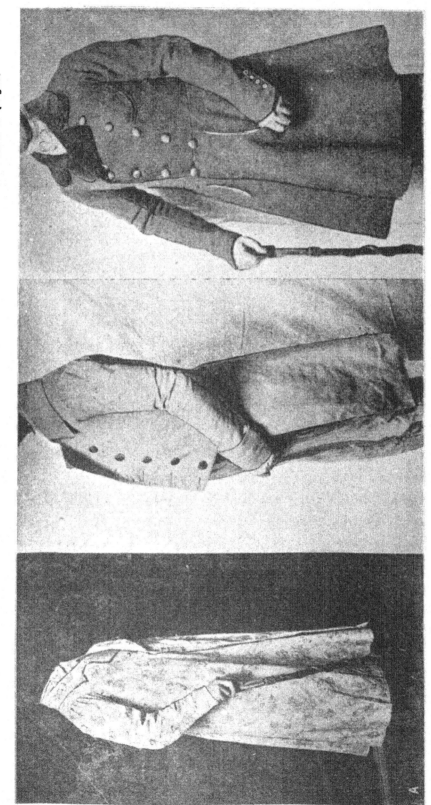

Pattern, see p. 313.

Pattern, see p. 307.

Pattern similar to p. 311.

Plate XXVI.—**(a)** Morning Coat of Chintz. 1825–45.   **(b)** Cloth Coat. 1808–20.   **(c)** Cloth Overcoat. 1820–35.

over collars and a wide-shaped lapel, and the lapel of the waistcoat was still brought outside. As these lapels on the coats became smaller and changed into a roll collar, they were cut into points at the breast, as seen in the illustrations.

The front of the coat cut away in a short square, rather high in the waist, which thus formed a long-tailed skirt; the fronts were made double-breasted, and were often fastened high up the lapel. The hip-pleats had gone round more to the back into a closely pressed fold, about three inches from the back-opening. Sleeves were gathered rather full in the shoulders, becoming very tight on the forearm, and were finished in a cuff, or buttoned cuff-shape. We also see that a short square coat without tails was worn over the longer one. Overcoats (or long-skirted coats) with a cape or capes, up to four, were worn all through this reign, both double and single breasted, sometimes with turn-up cuffs; but this mode was not frequently used, as a sewn-on cuff or cuff made in the sleeve was now worn, and began to take a curved shape well over the hand, with three buttons to fasten it on the outer sides.

247

Short double-breasted waistcoats continued much the same, but a round-shaped lapel appeared on many.

Very tight-fitting breeches were worn of the same 18th-century cut, and trousers began to gain favour; a fob of seals, &c., was always worn, coming from under the waistcoat.

Soft high boots with turn-down tops, and boots with longish brown tops set low on the leg. The top-boot with the pointed or oval-shaped front and tassel still held sway, and an oval-toed low shoe with or without small latchets was in use.

NINETEENTH CENTURY. GEORGE IV.
FEMALE.

The hair at this period was worn in plaits or curls gathered on top, and during the latter years was arranged into stiff loops set with a high comb; a group of curls was drawn to the sides of the face, the hair being mostly parted from the centre. Plumes were much used for head-dresses, and caps with gathered puffs and pointed frills. A high-crowned straw poke bonnet, tilted upwards, was still in form; but the prevailing mode was a silk

248

1809   1816   1820

1809   1807   1806

FIG. 110.

bonnet, with the brim curved in at the front, the sides being drawn together under the chin with a bow. The prevailing decoration was a group of feathers thrown forward or ribbon loops, and after this a large round hat, with a full gathered crown, arrived about 1827, or straw shapes, such as Fig. A, Plate XXVIII (see p. 259).

Dresses gradually assumed a longer waist, and a short pointed bodice made its appearance here and there from about 1822, when short stays began to return, and pointed belt corselets were frequent, though the waistband or sash was chiefly used. Short puffed sleeves of charming character and workmanship were sometimes set in a gauze sleeve, as in Fig. C, Plate XXIII (see p. 218). Spencers and pelisses had long sleeves coming from these short ones; they were rather full, and were caught at the wrist with a band. The upper sleeve gradually disappeared as the full-topped sleeves began to develop in size, about 1824; this fullness was often broken up into gathered parts, a tight cuff-piece usually finished at the wrist. The high set-up collars and neck-frills gave way to the flat capes about 1827, though the small ruffs were worn round the top of the high-

Plate XXVII.—Outdoor Silk Dress.　1825-35.

1820

1823

1822

1820

1822

1821

1828

1824

FIG. III.

necked capes to 1830. The gathered
shoulder began about 1823, and soon
became a marked feature; pointed or
scalloped frills and trimmings came into
favour from 1825, Fig. B, Plate XXIII (see
p. 218), and about 1827 the sloped appearance in the bodice began to be noticed as
the sleeves were set lower. The shoulders in
ball dresses were shown, and a gathered
Bertha of silk or lace was arranged round the
neck of bodice, Fig. D, Plate XXIV (see
p. 231), or this form was made in the pattern
as in Fig. C, Plate XXII (see p. 215). The
V-shaped piece from the centre of waist or
breast began to spread over the shoulders,
where it was opened, as in Fig. B, Plate XXII
(see p. 215). This V shape was often open
down to the waist, where it was filled in
with a centre-piece of embroidery. Skirts
were gradually set out fuller, with stiff-
flounced petticoats; they had various simple
or richly decorated borders and fronts, or
several small flounces, or one deep one
often with the edges cut into divers shapes.

I have striven to give good examples of
the marked styles in the various dated
illustrations, as well as the court train
to dress, Fig. A, Plate XXXIII (see p. 282),
which also comes into this time.

Shoes were rather round at the toes till near the end of the reign, when they took a square shape; a tiny rosette or bow was placed at the front of instep, and they were held by narrow ribbons, crossed and tied round the ankle. Boots lacing at the inside, with seam down the front, often had a toe-cap as in Fig. 5, Plate XXI (see p. 202); no heels were worn.

Light gauze scarves were usually carried, and very small fans besides the larger feather ones. Bags or sachets of the forms illustrated were painted or embroidered in ribbonwork, chenille, tulle, and coloured silks.

A few specimens of parasols are also given, and gloves and mittens were of the same character as in the latter part of the last reign.

The patterns given of some of the dresses shown in the plates will be useful as to the measurements of the increase in skirt-width and sleeves; one may also note the very pointed set-out of the breast, sometimes made with two gores, which only occurs in this reign. Muffs were usually of a large size, and a bow with long ends was often worn on the front.

The mode in beaver hats was most varied; high straight crowns with small brims, others tapering at the top with larger curled brims, or crowns enlarging at the top with almost straight small brims; a top-hat of straw is shown on page 309. A short-crowned hat was also worn. The hair was combed towards the front at either side, and the face shaven, with the exception of short side-whiskers.

A very high stock of black satin or linen surrounded the throat, with or without the points of collar showing, and a frilled shirt, often stiffly goffered.

Coats were very tight-fitting and mostly double-breasted, with long swallow-tailed skirts, or long full skirts; the waist was rather short, and the effect of coat-front round-breasted with a high turned-over collar finished in large lapels, which were often treated with velvets. The favourite colours for overcoats were greys, buffs, greens, and blues, and the edges were neatly finished with fine cord. The sleeves, rather full in the shoulder, became tight on the

254

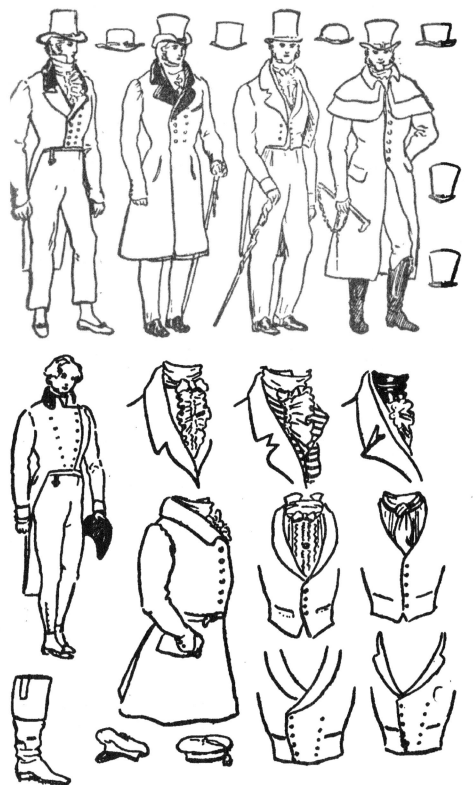

FIG. 112.—Period 1820–1840.

lower arm, coming to a curved shape well over the hand, and buttoned up the side. The pockets were frequently set at an angle, as in illustration, and a short round cape, or two, was seen on many overcoats. A short type of coat is seen about 1827, with a single roll collar.

Waistcoats mostly had a round-shaped lapel, and were often double-breasted and very shaped at the waist, which was set fairly high; a long opening allowed the frilled shirt-front full display. There were also waistcoats having no lapels, no pockets, or no cover-flap; the points of front were very small, being buttoned to the end, or, with the double-breasted shape, they were straight across.

Breeches were not so much worn as trousers of cloth, nankeen, drill, and fine white corduroy; these were usually fastened under the boots with a strap, others were looser and often worn short, well above the ankle. A very full type in the upper part peg-tops, was in fashion about 1820–25 amongst the dandies, and for evening dress, very close-fitting breeches to the knee, or just above the ankle, the latter being opened and buttoned up to the calf. Pince-nez were favoured, with a heavy

FIG. 113.—1830–1840.

R

black ribbon, generally worn tucked in the lapels of the waistcoat; and a fob of gold seals, &c., hung from the braces, below waistcoat pocket.

Shoes and short Wellington boots were chiefly worn, the former being low in the heel and very short in the tongue, which was almost covered by small latchets, either buckled or tied, the shape of the toe being rather round. The Hessian boots with curved front and tassel at the top were still worn.

NINETEENTH CENTURY. WILLIAM IV. FEMALE.

The hair still retained the high loops on top and the bunch of curls at the sides, poised by a back comb and set with flowers or feathers; there was also a great variety of fancy capes with pointed frills, some with long tie ends, and these are seen with most dresses, and were worn in conjunction with the hats. The favourite hat was a big, flat, circular form, generally tilted at one side, and decorated with bows, flowers, and feathers; a flat tam-o'-shanter shape was often worn with the riding-dress, sometimes with a large peak-shape in front, and straps

XXVIII.—(a) Silk Pelisse. 1820–30.
(b) Cotton Dress. 1830–40. (Pattern, see p. 343).
(c) Silk Spencer and Cape. 1818-27 (Pattern, see p. 324).

FIG. 114.—1828-1836.

under the chin. The large poke-bonnet also kept the front as flat and round as possible, with a high crown tilted upward in order to set over the hair loops.

The bodice began with a very pointed front and very low neck off the shoulders, tuck-ins of fine embroidery, and capes or fichus of the same, covered the shoulders, often three deep. The pointed bodice only lasted for a few years, when the waist-band again became the favourite. The sleeves were very large at the shoulders, diminishing at the wrist, but soon took a big round form, sometimes tightly pleated into quarters before 1835. We then get the huge sleeve gathered at the wrist, and often falling below it; this again tightened on the forearm, and we note a tendency to tighter sleeves coming in before 1837, neatly gathered well down the shoulder. The evening-dress sleeve was a large puff, set out by stiffening to a flat wide effect. Very wide epaulet collars were seen on most dresses, meeting in a V shape at the waist, with a filling of lace in the front, and many bodices were elaborately gathered, and some of the sleeves were also gathered into puffs all down the arm.

FIG. 115.—1830–1840.

The skirts were set out very full over stiff flounced petticoats, and were worn rather short; as a rule they were trimmed with one or two flounces, which were handsomely decorated, and a short polonaise is occasionally seen. There were many interesting trimmings of gauze, flowers, and bows; while silk-flowered gauze over dresses made some charming effects.

Heavy mantles and capes or pelisses began to be braided, and rather strong colours were in general taste.

The hand-bags were of a curved form and generally bore heavy tassels. Very small fans and round fans were attractive, and bouquet-holders of gilt, with pearl handles, became the thing to carry.

Shoes were of the low sandal type, fastened by crossed elastic, with very square toes, and a tiny rosette or bow on the front; boots to the ankle were now in fashion, mostly lacing at the inside, and having a long toe-cap, sometimes with a small rosette at the top of this or a tassel at front of the top of the boot.

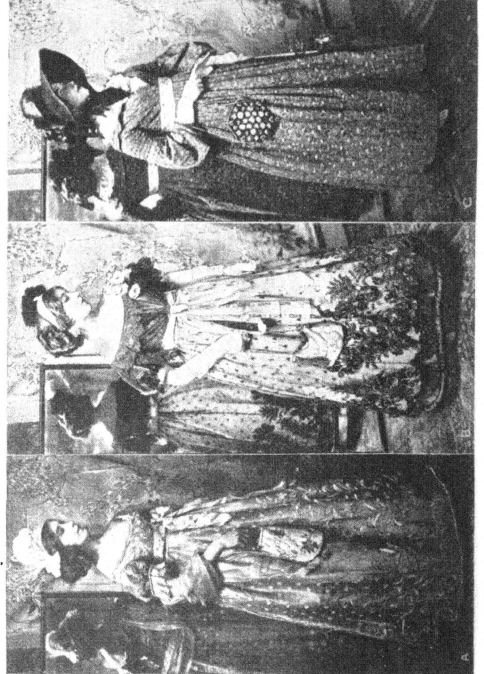

Plate XXIX. (a) Embroidered Silk Gauze Dress. 1820-30. (b) Gauze Dress with Appliqued Design. 1825-35.

NINETEENTH CENTURY. WILLIAM IV.
MALE.

The hair was worn rather full in curls at the sides or on top, parted at the left side, besides being occasionally parted at the centre.   Side whiskers, curved forward, still continued, and a short trimmed beard was now worn round under the chin by many, moustaches also made their first appearance at the end of this reign.   Top-hats were high and straight, but many still adhered to the tapered crown and larger brim.

The same plain stocks of black satin continued, with or without a front bow, and a soft pleated or frilled shirt-front.

The coats were similar to the last reign : the chief differences being an increase in the length of the waist, wider tails, and large lapels of a similar cut : velvet collars and cuffs were much worn, and the waist was still made tight.   A coat with a square skirt as in Fig. 116 is seen for the first time, and the swallow-tailed coat was worn not quite so long.   A lower opening to the waistcoat was generally seen in evening attire, which sometimes had but four small buttons, while more of the single-breasted type were in use, with and without lapels.

Very tight trousers to the ankle buttoned up to the calf continued, or plain trousers were held by straps under the boot; twill, corduroy, or nankeen were both strapped or free at the ankle and rather short. Knee-breeches were still worn by many for evening dress, and long Italian capes with overcapes and high turn-over collars were fashionable, besides the very full-skirted greatcoat.

Boots and shoes were square at the toes and rather long and narrow, the shoes having a bow or buckle. Short Wellington boots continued much in use, also spats.

Fobs of gold seals, &c., were worn, and eye-glasses attached to a black ribbon is a noticeable feature.

NINETEENTH CENTURY. VICTORIA.
FEMALE.

The hair was parted in the centre and tightened in a top setting of plaits, with side curls over the ears. This mode was retained by many till the fifties, but the top plaits began to be set lower at the back, and the same flat parted hair was

264

FIG. 116.—1840–1860.

brought in a curved shape to the front of the ears, often in a small plait, allowing the ear to show, or in a plaited knot at either side; about 1850 it was waved, parted, and simply curved from the forehead over the ears in a fuller manner, sometimes being turned under to increase the side fullness, while the back hair was arranged lower down the neck. In the sixties the hair was waved and caught behind in ringlets or was bunched into the hideous chignons, which are seen till about 1880.

The variety of caps and hats is too alarming to deal with, and baffles comprehensible description, so it is best for the student to dip into the hundreds of illustrations through this period in the *Ladies' Magazine*, *Punch*, the *Illustrated London News*, or the *Ladies' Treasury* for the later styles.

The straw bonnet with a straighter poke front was favoured till 1850, when the front became considerably reduced in size and fitted closely round the face. The larger brimmed bonnets had a little frill by the ears, and the tight-brimmed bonnet often had the frill all round with a flower also tucked in effectively to the wearer's taste, and we see this favoured till the

Plate XXX.—(*a*) Printed Silk Bodice. 1840-50. (*Pattern, see* p. 320.)
(*b*) Gathered Linen Bodice. 1837-47.
(*c*) Silk Bodice and Bertha. 1845-55.

FIG. 117.—1845-1855.

seventies. In the fifties a large flat Leg-horn hat with a small crown was in evi-dence, the brim dipping back and front, decorated with feathers or bows, and a three-cornered French hat with feathers set in the brim came in with revival of the 18th-century style about 1860. A small bowler hat and a very small "pork-pie" hat appears in the late sixties, and a tiny-shaped bonnet of a curved form during the seventies.

At the beginning of this long reign we find the pointed bodice with a normal length of waist has really come to stay, though many dresses retain the waistband till the fifties, and there is such a con-fusion of styles at that time, it is difficult to arrange a sequence. From the 18th century fashions became more complicated in the greater variety of design, each over-lapping the other, and several distinct forms of character come and go during this long reign. I do not envy the person who undertakes the chronology of our present period.

At the commencement in 1837 the huge sleeves gathered at the wrist were still in evidence, especially as a gauze oversleeve to evening attire, and they continued thus to the fifties, but very large sleeves were really dying out and the usual reaction was setting in; the full-shouldered sleeve had turned a somersault and was neatly gathered tight from the shoulder to the elbow, the fullness falling on the forearm, and this was gathered into a tight setting or wristband. The V-shaped front to the bodice was kept in many dresses by a collar or two tapering from the shoulders to the waist, the fullness of the breast often being tightly gathered at the shoulders, besides a few inches in the front point of the bodice. A very plain tight-fitting sleeve became fashionable, and on most of these we find a small upper sleeve or a double one as shown in A, Plate XXX (see p. 266); this was sometimes opened at the outer side. These sleeves continued till about 1852. In 1853 a bell-shaped sleeve is noticed in ordinary dress, and this continued in various sizes till 1875, reaching its fuller shape about 1864. These types of sleeves were usually worn over a tight one or a full lawn sleeve gathered at the wrist; most bodices with this sleeve were closely fitted and high in the neck, the waist often being cut into small tabs. We also notice for a few years in the early fifties the

269

deeper part of the bell curved to the front of the arm, giving a very ugly appearance. A close-fitting jacket also came into evidence till about 1865 with tight sleeves and cuffs, sometimes with a little turndown collar and a longer skirt as in Fig. C, Plate XXXIII (see p. 282). This particularly fine embroidered specimen, in imitation of the 18th-century style, is interestingly cut away short at the back to allow for better setting on the crinoline. There is another type of sleeve seen about 1848, of a plain, full, square cut; these became varied in shape, being opened up the side and generally trimmed with wide braids. This clumsy character is seen up to 1878, the later ones being fuller in cut. Zouave jackets were occasionally worn in the forties and later in the early sixties, when the wide corselet belt was again favoured. Skirts at the beginning of the reign were fully set out on drill petticoats, stiff flounces, and even whalebone, so it was hardly " a great effect " when the crinoline appeared about 1855, though a furious attack was made against it at first; this undersetting developed to its fullest extent between 1857 and 1864, and many dresses in the early sixties

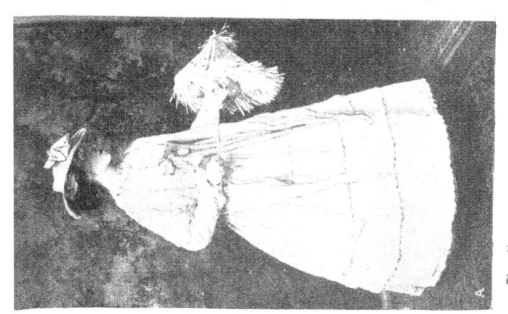

were also worn short, showing the high
boots of this period. At first the crinoline
was slightly held back from the front by
ties, and again in the sixties it was often
kept with a straight front, the fullness
being held to the back, till the appearance
of the bustle brought in another shape.

FIG. 118.—Dress improvers, 1865–1875.

The skirts were now pulled in tight to
the front of the figure and bunched up
at the back, with a train or shaped flounced
pieces overlapping each other caught up
under the bustle, as in Fig. B, Plate XXXIII
(see p. 282).

Mantles of a cumbersome type and shot-
silk capes with long pointed fronts were

271

worn, often heavily fringed, the former also being mostly decorated with braided designs. Large Paisley shawls were much used all through this reign, besides the cape and hood with its fine tassels which became very fashionable in the sixties.

Gloves and mittens are seen both long and short, the latter often beautifully embroidered on the back in the French style. Hand-bags were often carried, of which examples are given in the plates of a variety of shapes; the favourite materials for their make were velvets and silks decorated with bullion, sequins, braids, needlework, and beads, and these bags were richly set in gilt, silver, or steel mounts.

Parasols were still heavily fringed, and were of the usual shapes. A very small one was carried in the carriages, and are even seen on the ladies' driving whips.

Shoes continued in the same heelless sandal character to the sixties for evening wear, but from the forties most outdoor shoes had a heel and large rosettes. With the seventies came round toes with a low round front and bow, and high shaped heels came to stay till the present day. Boots of white satin, kid, or coloured silks were chiefly worn till the seventies,

272

reaching just above the ankle, laced up the inner side, but many wore elastic sides from the fifties; the toes of these were rather square, and a toe-cap and front seam was made in many of this type. In the forties a tight rosette was sometimes placed low down towards the toes, and later, a huge bow was sewn on the front. High boots buttoned towards the side and very much shaped, with pointed round toes and high heels were sometimes laced and finished with a pair of tassels. Spats were always fashionable through this period.

NINETEENTH CENTURY. VICTORIA.
MALE.

The same modes of doing the hair re- mained till the sixties, parted at one side and worn rather long and waved, with the side whiskers or beard all round the chin. The side whiskers were allowed to grow long between fifty-five and seventy, and full beards also became fashionable, while the hair was parted in the centre from front to back and flattened on the forehead.

The favourite top-hat still reigned supreme, many of which retained the tapered top and large curled brim till about 1855, and a bell shape was frequently seen in the fifties, but the real straight chimney shape was seen throughout till the eighties, with a rather narrow brim, and often of white or fawn-coloured cloth. The bowler hat increased in appreciation, being of a short type, with smallish brim. A short flat felt hat, with rather straight brim, also came into favour from the fifties; little round caps and caps with ear-flaps, for travelling, &c., were also in general use.

The frock-coat kept the rather tight sleeves and tight waist, and full square skirt, with back pockets, also a deep lapel, sometimes with a velvet collar, and small cuffs; a breast-pocket was often placed on the left side, and in the fifties the type of morning coat with rounded-off fronts at the skirt appeared, also a small collar and lapel. Square-cut jackets and tweed suits similar to our present shapes, but heavier in cut and with braided edges, were much in use. Velvet or fur-trimmed overcoats, and heavy travelling-coats, also capes and Inverness capes, were all in vogue.

Waistcoats became buttoned higher in the

neck, and the stock-collar was supplanted in the sixties by a turn-down collar, and small tie or loose bow; many still affected the black stock and pointed collar to the seventies, when a high round collar began to appear.

Coloured and fancy waistcoats were much worn till the eighties, and evening dress was similar to the present cut, with slight differences in the length of lapels and waistcoat front.

The trousers were made with the front flap till they were buttoned down the front about 1845, and side pockets became general. Braids may be noted down the sides in the fifties, and are seen now and then all through the reign, while large plaids and stripes were highly esteemed.

Short Wellington boots were chiefly preferred up to the sixties, and trouser-straps and spats were fashionable all through the reign. The heavier lace-up boot came in during the fifties, and a very shaped type of fashion appeared in the sixties.

Having now completed the general survey of Costume, the following pages are given up to the cut and measurements of various antique garments.

PATTERNS OF VARIOUS REIGNS FROM ANTIQUE COSTUME

WITH NOTES AND MEASUREMENTS

Patterns of Various Reigns from Antique Costume

I HAVE striven to gather as many representative patterns of dress types and accessories as possible, and also give many measurements from the various examples, when I have been unable to obtain a complete pattern. The character of cut and proportion is the essential point in the study of dress design, and the intimate knowledge of periods. When seeing a collection of patterns, one is astonished at the great variety in cut used to arrive at the different bodice types. Several patterns of single pieces are given, as it aids one to find the fellow-part; for example, the photo of a back given in Fig. C, Plate III (see p. 55), will go with the front cut on page 290; even though these two pieces did not belong to the same body, the cut is seen from

276

which to design the missing part. Often a small piece is wanting for the top of the shoulder, which can easily be supplied to fill the sleeve measurement. The types of trimmings in the different centuries will soon be acquired by a careful student, and the proportions of patterns will be valued for gaining the character. I believe with this collection one could get the true effects of any style of dress seen in the period prints. The drawings are mostly scaled for the half, and the measurement, in inches, will be found by dots on the top of the collotypes, and by a marked line on the pattern pages.

One must note, with the 18th-century dress, the sleeve cuffs can be changed, so I give, on page 300, a full-size measurement of the elbow-cuff seen in Fig. A, Plate XVI (see p. 167), and a deeper one of this style is seen on Fig. C, Plate XII (see p. 135), gathered seven times at the elbow. The plain square type was pleated in the front as given on page 300, and a variety of this character is shown on Fig. B, Plate XV (see p. 154). Though many patterns may be found remarkable in proportions, an allowance is often to be made for the undersetting, as well as for the thick, straight corsets worn to the end of the 18th century.

I give several specimens of quilting on petticoats of the 18th century, which will probably be found useful to artists; the measurement is also given of their circumference, which attained similar proportions to those set on the Victorian crinolines, going 3 to 4 yards round: four 18th century ones measured 100, 114, 116, 120 inches, and they are often 1 inch longer at the sides, to allow for setting over the panniers; a pattern is given on pages 213 and 332. The embroidered pockets on page 300 were worn in pairs at the sides on the petticoats, and only showed when the dress was looped up. The extra lawn sleeves, given on page 287, show how precious the superfine linen was held, with its superb gathered work, lace ruffles, and often fine embroidery; these pieces could be looked after with special care in the laundry, and could be tacked, pinned, or buttoned on when required.

The 16th and 17th century collars were mostly attached to the chemise or shirt, as is seen in many of the old prints. On page 289 I give examples of shape of the various stomachers, which will be found

278

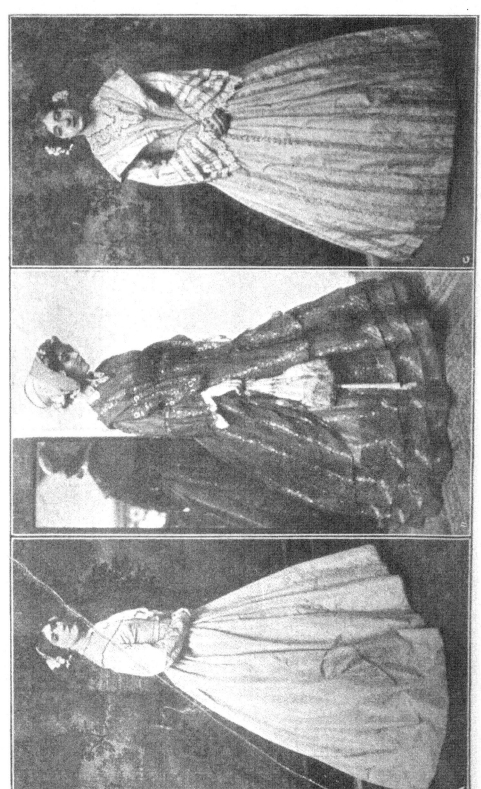

Pattern, see p. 344.

Pattern, see p. 346.

Plate XXXII.— (a) Silk Dress, 1860-70.

useful for getting the characteristic proportions. The scarves worn round the body of the 17th century cavaliers were from 2 feet 3 inches wide to 3 feet 6 inches, and from 8 feet 6 inches to 7 feet in length.

The stocking top, Fig. C, Plate VI (see p. 74), is probably of similar proportions to the woollen one in the Victoria and Albert Museum, on which the bell-top circumference is 36 inches, and the full length of stocking 38 inches. On page 285 a cap of three pieces is given; their real design is at present unknown, but I trust the Museum authorities may soon discover their placing, for many of these pieces are in existence, and this set in my collection is impressed with a beautiful pattern. The bodice, Fig A, Plate X (see p. 292), should have been set on a stiff-fronted corset to give it the straight style, as it is charmingly proportioned and clean in outline. I have also measured a short circular cloak of the early 17th century, which is 34 inches in diameter, with a square collar 10 inches deep; and another cape of the late 16th century, 40 inches in diameter. On page 290 will be found the smaller tabs which are placed round the jerkin, with a deep front point, as in

279

Patterns of
Various
Reigns
from
Antique
Costume

Fig. A, Plate VIII*a* (see p. 103); the collar of this type often rises $2\frac{3}{4}$ inches in the front to 3 inches at the back, in order to carry the stiff ruff or deep turned-down collar. Tabs of the smallest dimensions, in the earlier Elizabeth and James character, generally have six pieces from front to the middle of the back, which are from 2 to 3 inches deep. The epaulets are made in small stiff tabs, caught together in two places only, and so have plenty of give in the shoulder movements; they run to $2\frac{1}{4}$ inches at the widest part, and do not continue right under the arm. Fig. D, Plate V (see p. 71), has the middle seam of the back open from the waist to within 2 inches of the collar, which is noticeable on many of the later Charles I coats. Long aprons are conspicuous through the 17th century, and one measured was 42 inches wide, gathered to 15 inches at the waist; they were decorated with three bands of embroidered insertion down the front, with a 3-inch plain border, edged with small lace; this is typical in character of design, as is also the same style of linen cape seen on a figure, page 159. A similar one, lent by Sir Robert Filmer, is at the Victoria and Albert Museum; also a cap, of which I give a pattern, A, page 285. The smaller type of embroidered aprons of the late 17th and 18th centuries measure 40 inches wide, 19½ inches deep, with the centre dipping to 17¾ inches; another shape is 26 inches wide, 18 inches in centre, and 13½ inches on sides. The bodice, with deep skirt, Fig. B, Plate XVIII (see p. 183), is a type seen all through the 18th century, both longer and shorter in the skirt. The pattern of the 17th-century breeches is interesting as regards the cut, the upper part being kept plain, otherwise the gathered fullness would have disturbed the set of the jerkin tabs; the band of these breeches has six hooks either side to back, which fasten to eyes on an under flap sewn on body of jerkin. The epaulet on this pattern is only a ¾-inch piece, braided with two narrow braids, and the bows on tabs are of ribbon, 1½ inches wide.

The three patterns of capes given on pages 349, 350 will be found useful, as they are simple and very typical of the Victorian times, long shawls being otherwise much used. The fullness of the Elizabethan overdress seen on B, Plate II (see p. 42), is 66 inches to the back seam, and the

Patterns of
Various
Reigns
from
Antique
Costume

Fig. C, on the same plate, is 47 inches. The "jump," or jacket, Fig. A, Plate III (see p. 55), is 100 inches round, the fullness of the sleeve 13 inches, and the length of back 32 inches. An over-tunic of the early 17th century is interesting to examine, though it is a specimen of German costume.

Pattern, see p. 329.

Plate XXXIII.—(a) Silk Dress with Court Train. 1828-38.   (b) Silk Afternoon Dress. 1872-78.   (c) Silk Coat and Skirt. 1855-65,

PATTERNS TO SCALE

For Detailed List, see page 353.

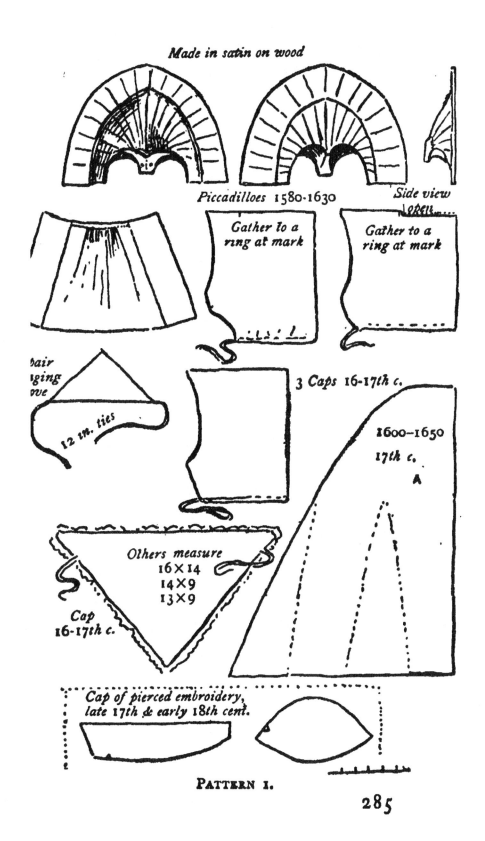

Made in satin on wood

Piccadilloes 1580-1630

Side view
open

Gather to a
ring at mark

Gather to a
ring at mark

3 Caps 16-17th c.

hair
iging
ve

12 in. ties

1600-1650

17th c.

A

Others measure
16×14
14×9
13×9

Cap
16-17th c.

Cap of pierced embroidery,
late 17th & early 18th cent.

PATTERN 1.

285

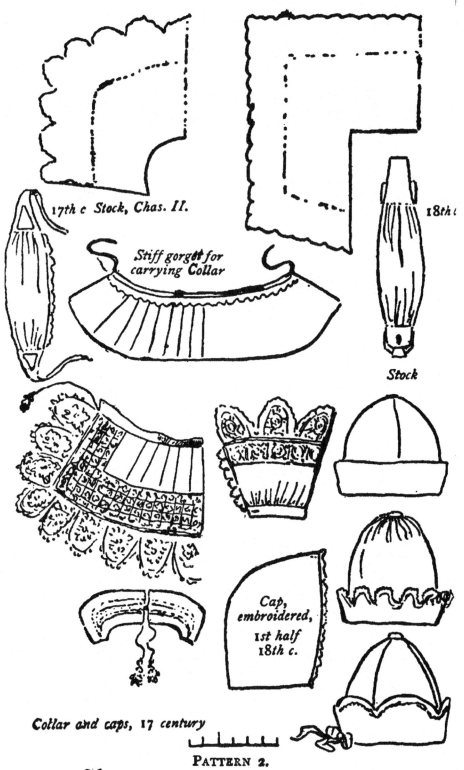

17th c Stock, Chas. II.

18th c

Stiff gorget for carrying Collar

Stock

Cap,
embroidered,
1st half
18th c.

Collar and caps, 17 century

PATTERN 2.

286

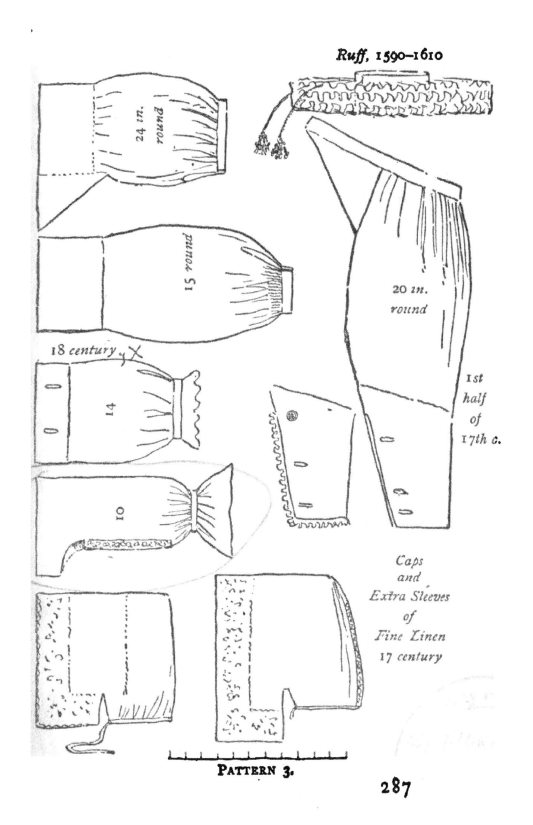

Ruff, 1590–1610

24 in. round

15 round

18 century

14

20 in. round

10

1st half of 17th c.

Caps and Extra Sleeves of Fine Linen 17 century

PATTERN 3.

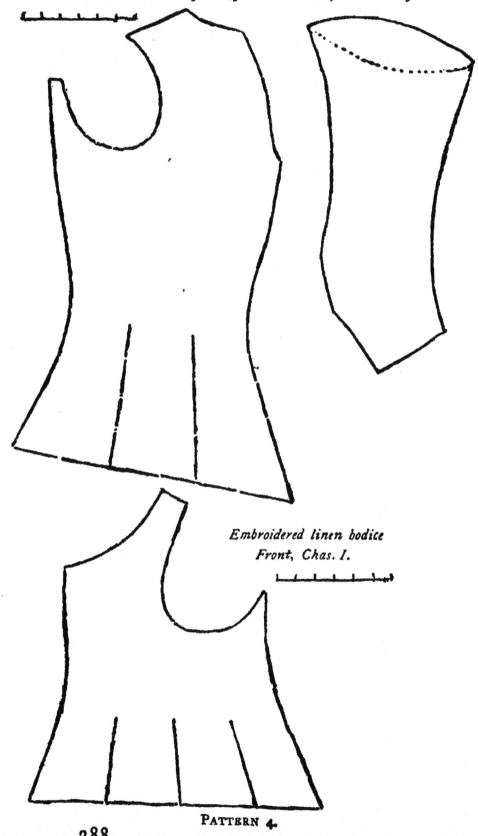

Embroidered linen jacket, front and sleeve, 16th century

Embroidered linen bodice
Front, Chas. I.

PATTERN 4.

Elizabethan jerkin of punched leather.

*Gold embroidered
stomacher,
about
1600-30*

1660-
1689

1690-
1730

1680-
1730

PATTERN 5.

T

289

PATTERNS TO SCALE

For Detailed List, see page 353.

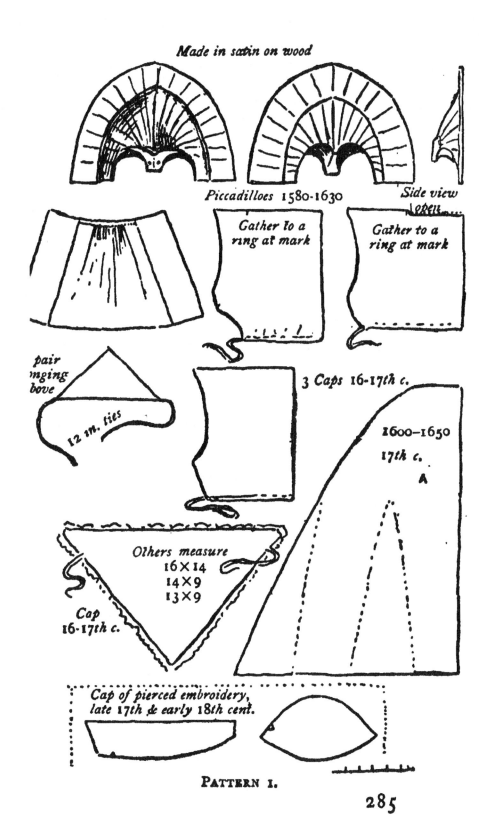

Made in satin on wood

Piccadilloes 1580-1630

Side view open

Gather to a ring at mark

Gather to a ring at mark

pair nging bove

12 in. ties

3 Caps 16-17th c.

1600–1650

17th c.

A

Others measure
16 × 14
14 × 9
13 × 9

Cap
16-17th c.

Cap of pierced embroidery,
late 17th & early 18th cent.

PATTERN I.

285

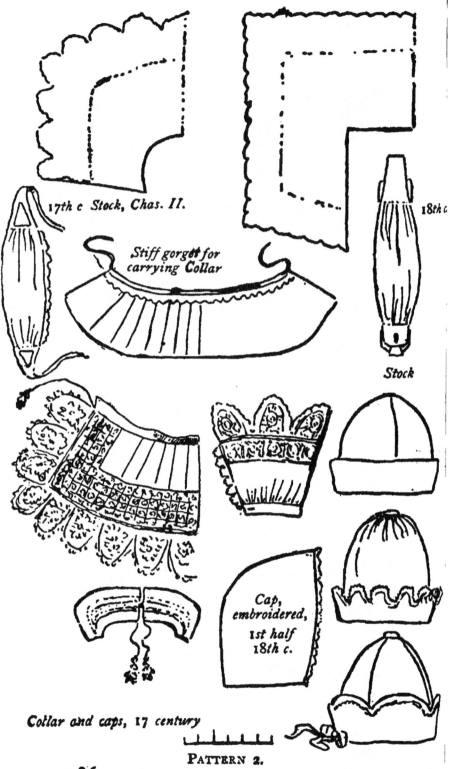

17th c Stock, Chas. II.

18th c

Stiff gorget for carrying Collar

Stock

Cap,
embroidered,
1st half
18th c.

Collar and caps, 17 century

PATTERN 2.

286

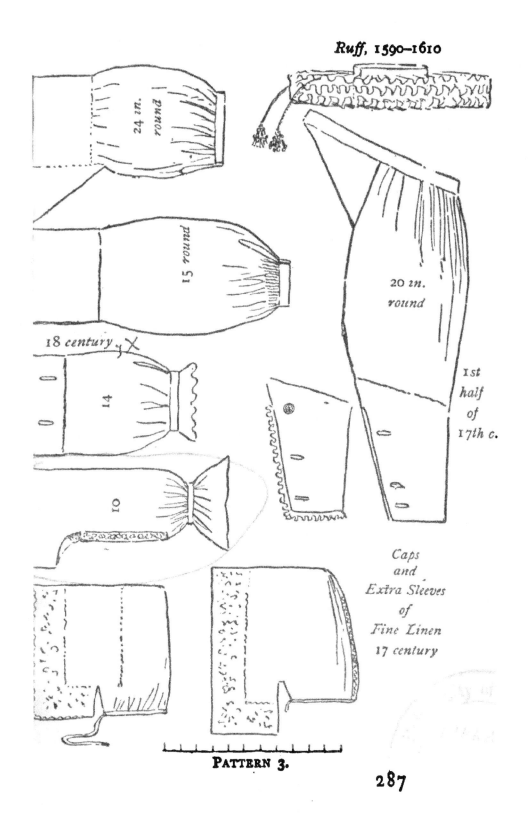

Ruff, 1590–1610

24 in. round

15 round

20 in. round

18 century

14

1st half of 17th c.

10

Caps and Extra Sleeves of Fine Linen 17 century

PATTERN 3.

287

Embroidered linen jacket, front and sleeve, 16th century

Embroidered linen bodice
Front, Chas. I.

PATTERN 4.

Elizabethan jerkin of punched leather.

Gold embroidered stomacher, about 1600-30

1660-
1689

1690-
1730

1680-
1730

PATTERN 5.

T

289

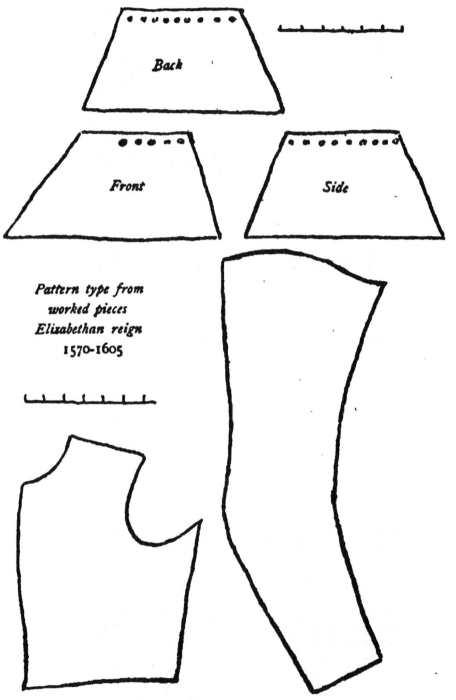

Set of tabs for male jerkin, 17 cent.

Back

Front

Side

Pattern type from
worked pieces
Elizabethan reign
1570-1605

PATTERN 6.

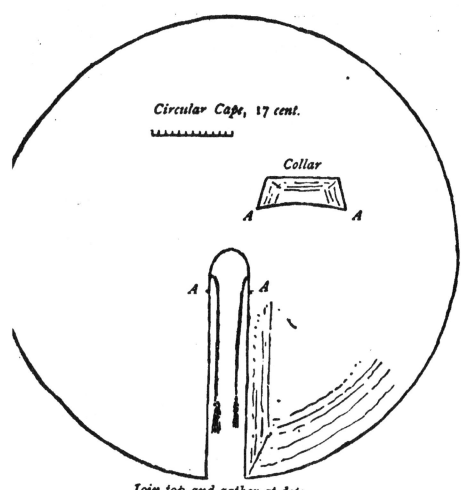

Circular Cape, 17 *cent.*

Collar

A   A

A   A

Join top and gather at dots.

Cap, 1580–1630.

PATTERN 7.

291

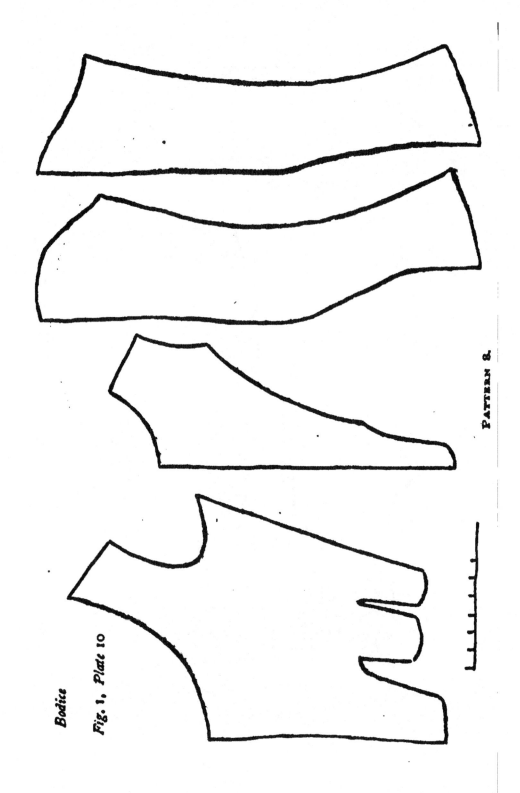

Bodice

Fig. 1, Plate 10

PATTERN 8.

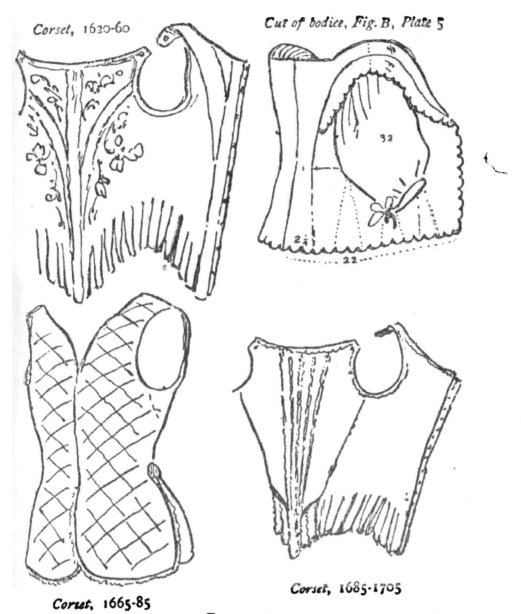

Corset, 1620-60

Cut of bodice, Fig. B, Plate 5

Corset, 1665-85

Corset, 1685-1705

PATTERN 9.

293

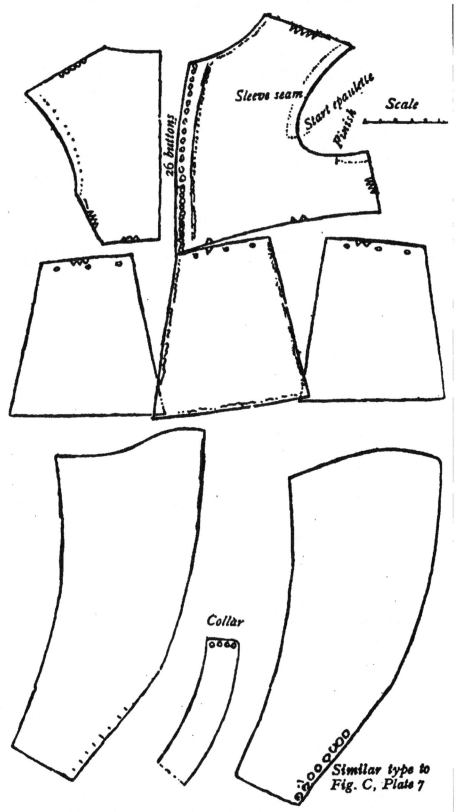

26 buttons

Sleeve seam

Start epaulette

Finish

Scale

Collar

Similar type to
Fig. C, Plate 7

Jerkin of white quilted satin
See page opposite for Breeches of same, 1620–1640. Victoria
and Albert Museum, Kensington.

PATTERN 10.

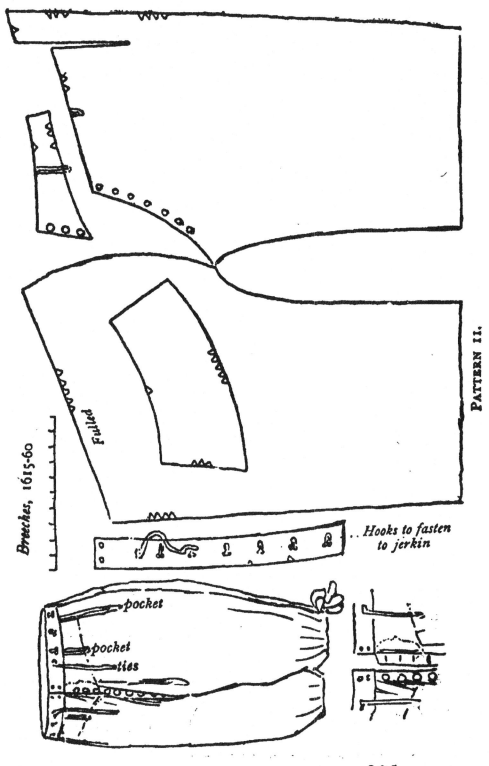

Breeches, 1615-60

Fulled

Hooks to fasten
to jerkin

PATTERN II.

pocket

pocket

ties

295

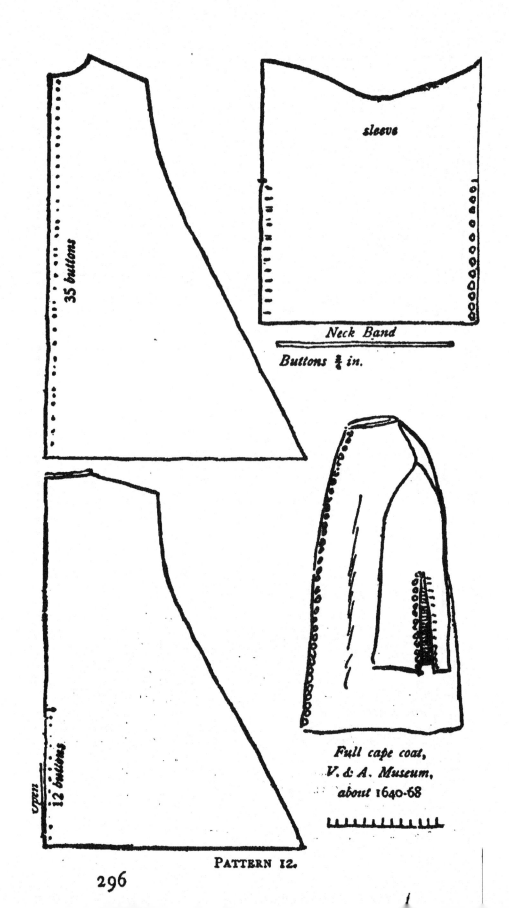

35 buttons

sleeve

Neck Band

Buttons ⅜ in.

12 buttons

open

Full cape coat,
V. & A. Museum,
about 1640-68

PATTERN 12.

296

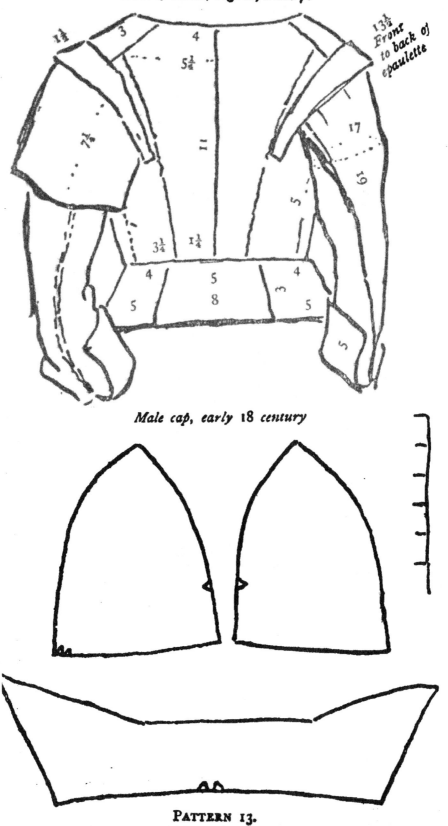

Back of bodice, Fig. B, Plate 7.

1½ 3 4

5¼

13½
Front
to back of
epaulette

7⅝

17

19

=

5

3¼ 1¼

4 5 4

5 8 3 5

5

Male cap, early 18 century

PATTERN 13.

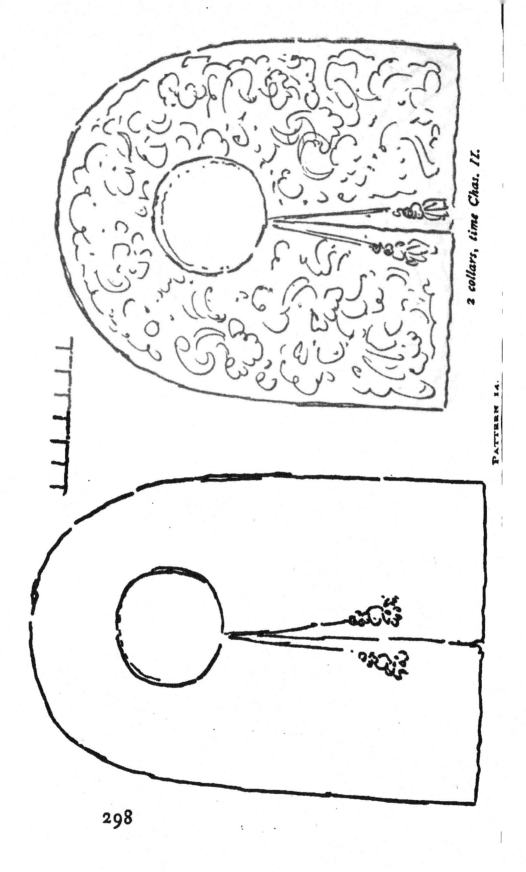

2 collars, time Chas. II.

PATTERN 14.

298

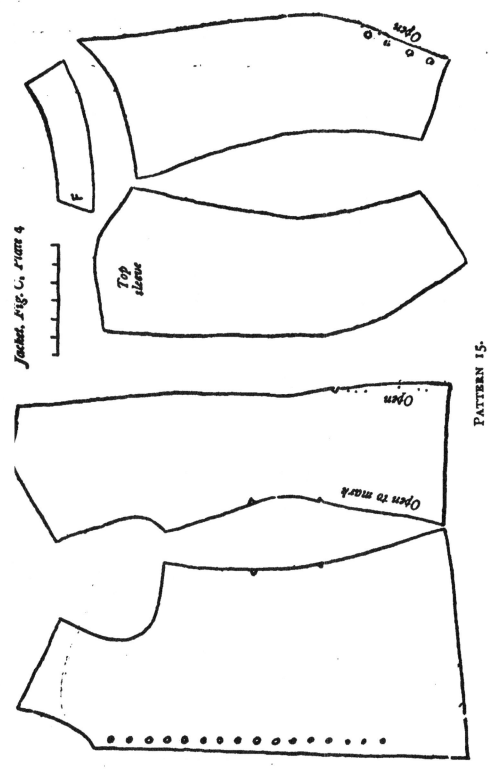

Jacket, Fig. C, Plate 4

Top sleeve

Open

Open

Open to mark

PATTERN 15.

299

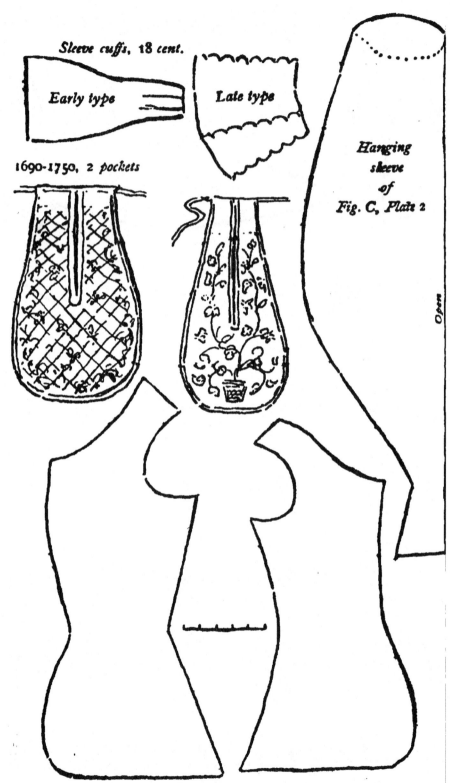

Sleeve cuffs, 18 cent.

Early type

Late type

1690-1750, 2 pockets

Hanging
sleeve
of
Fig. C, Plate 2

Open

Embroidered bodice fronts, early 18 century

PATTERN 16.

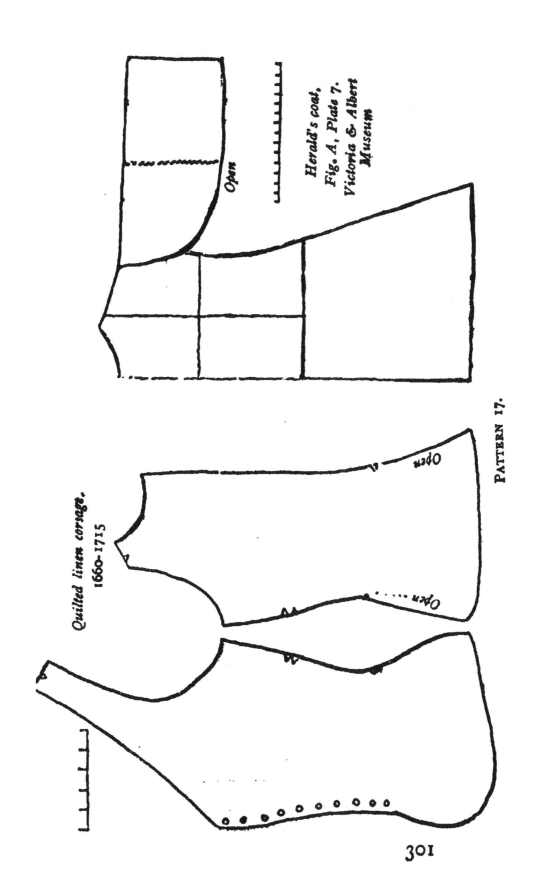

Herald's coat.
Fig. A, Plate 7.
Victoria & Albert
Museum

Open

Quilted linen corsage.
1660-1715

Open

Open

PATTERN 17.

301

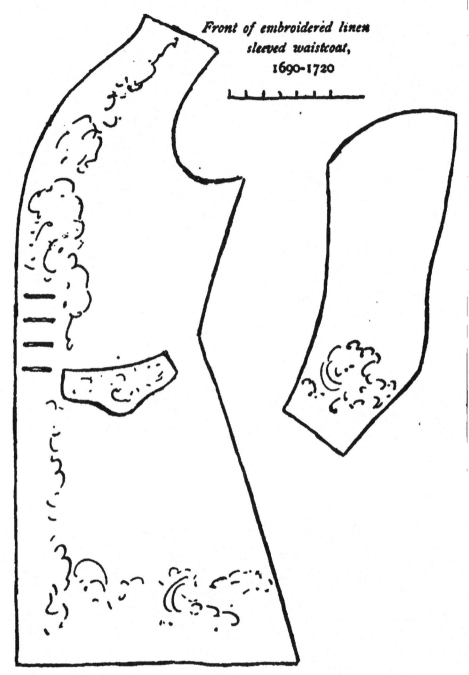

Front of embroidered linen
sleeved waistcoat,
1690-1720

Victoria and Albert Museum
PATTERN 18.

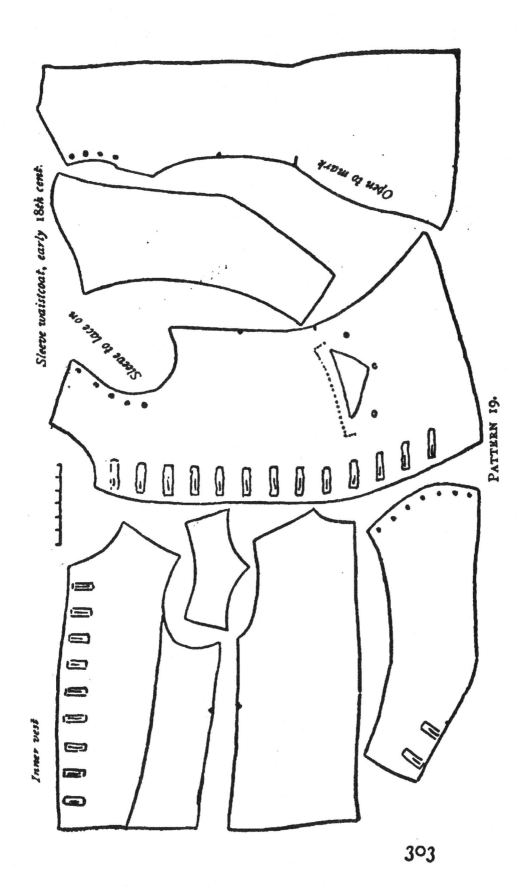

Sleeve waistcoat, early 18th cent.

Open to mark

Sleeve to lace on

Inner vest

PATTERN 19.

303

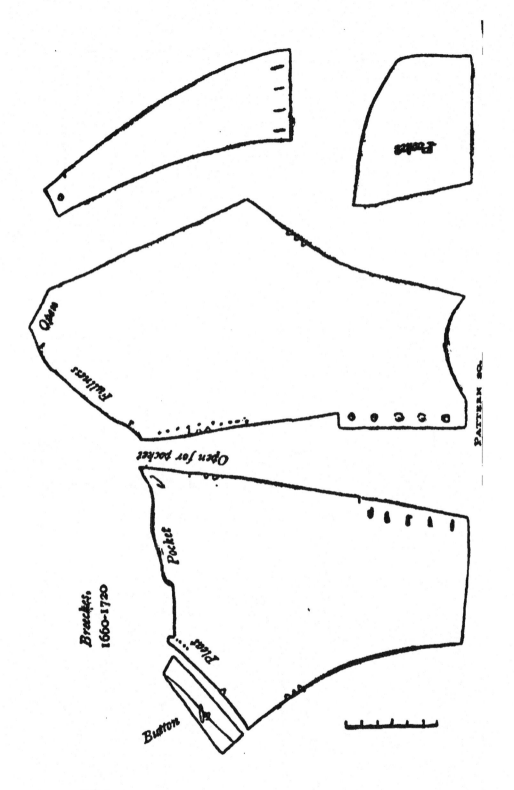

Breeches,
1660-1720

Open

Fullness

Open for pocket

Pocket

Pleat

Button

Probe

PATTERN 89.

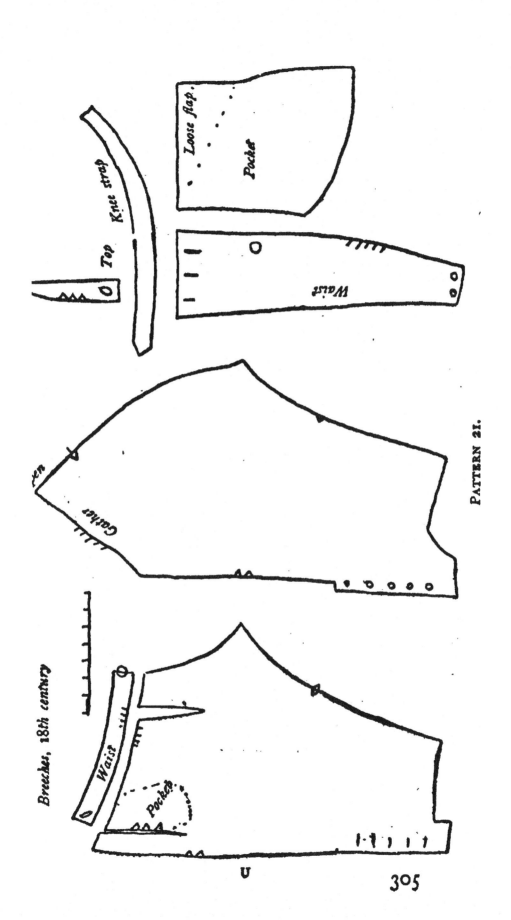

Loose flap.

Pocket

Top

Knee strap

Waist

PATTERN 21.

Gather

Breeches, 18th century

Waist

Pockets

U

305

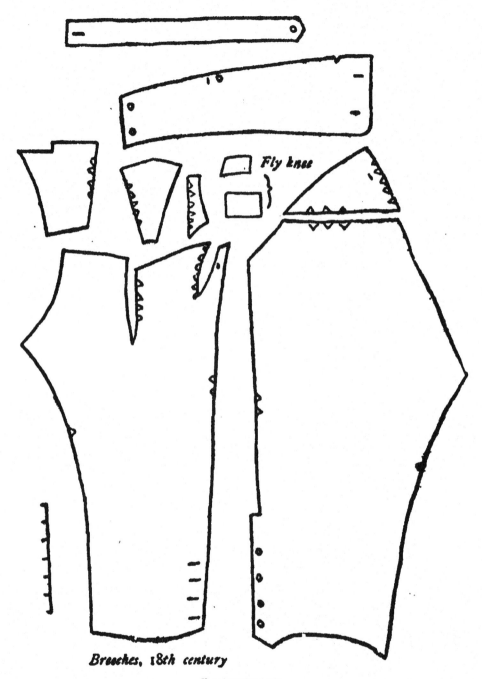

Fly knee

Breeches, 18th century

PATTERN 22.

306

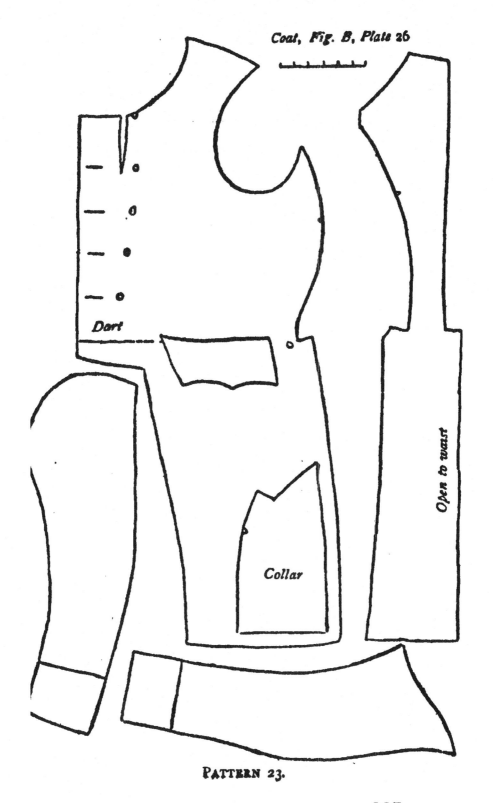

Coat, Fig. B, Plate 26

Dart

Open to waist

Collar

PATTERN 23.

307

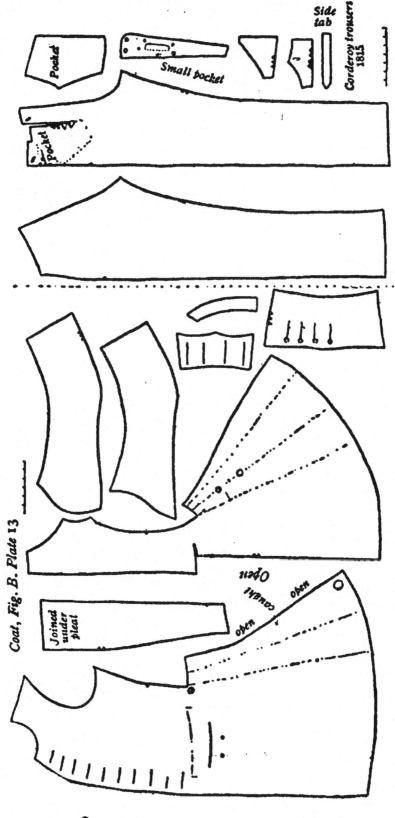

Pocket

Small pocket

Side tab

Corderoy trousers 1815

Pocket

Coat, Fig. B. Plate 13

Joined under pleat

Open

cauchi

open

open

PATTERN 24.

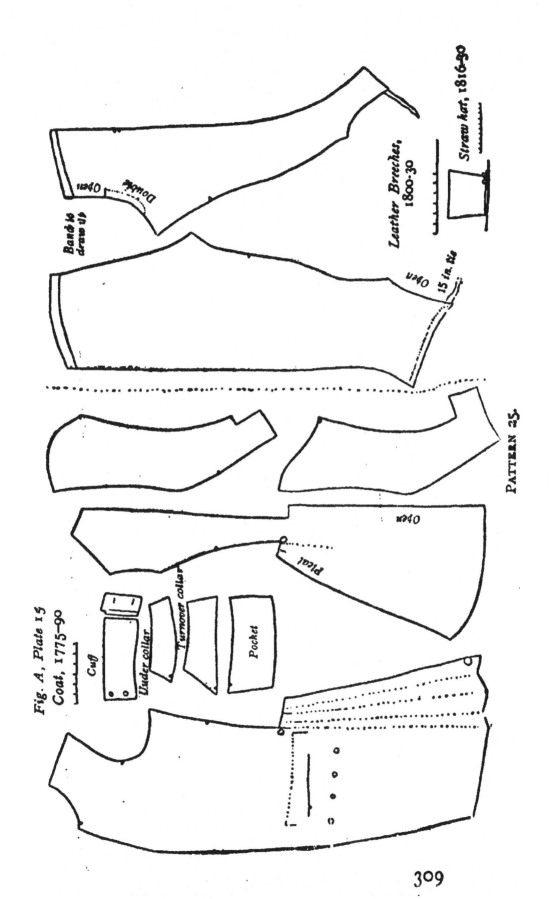

Fig. A, Plate 15
Coat, 1775-90

Cuff

Under collar

Turnover collar

Pocket

Open

Pleat

PATTERN 25.

Band to
draw up

Open

Double

Open

15 in. Me

Leather Breeches,
1800-30

Straw hat, 1816-30

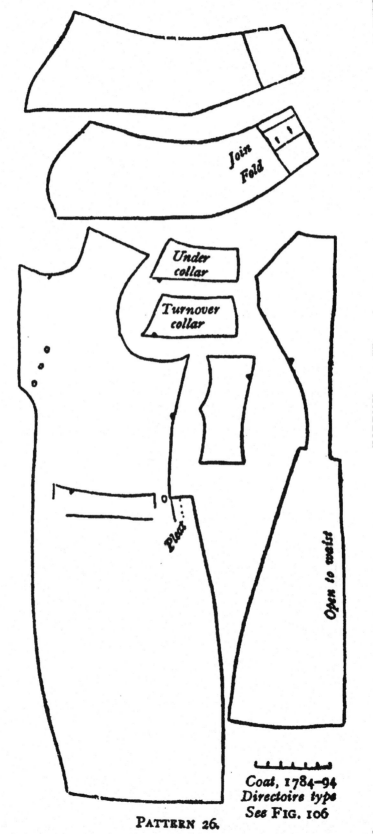

Join
Fold

Under
collar

Turnover
collar

Pleat

Open to waist

Coat, 1784-94
Directoire type
See FIG. 106

PATTERN 26.

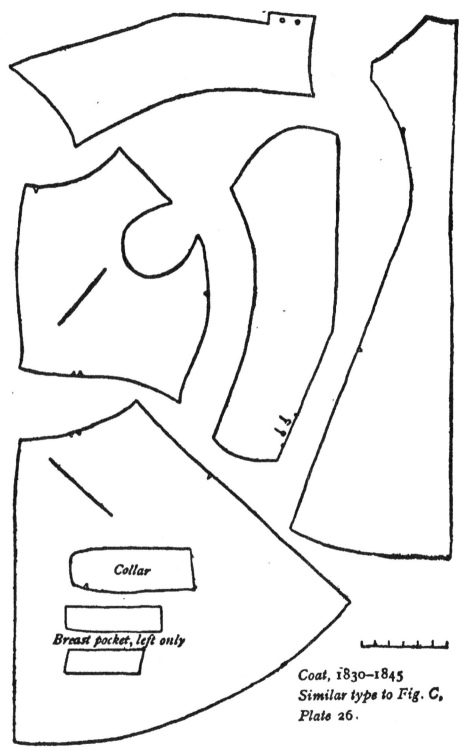

Collar

Breast pocket, left only

Coat, 1830–1845
Similar type to Fig. C,
Plate 26.

PATTERN 27.

311

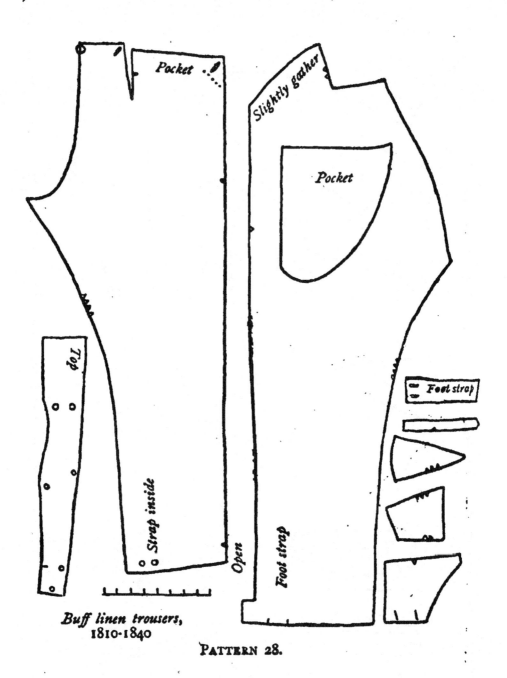

Pocket

Slightly gather

Pocket

Top

Foot strap

Strap inside

Open

Foot strap

Buff linen trousers,
1810-1840

PATTERN 28.

312

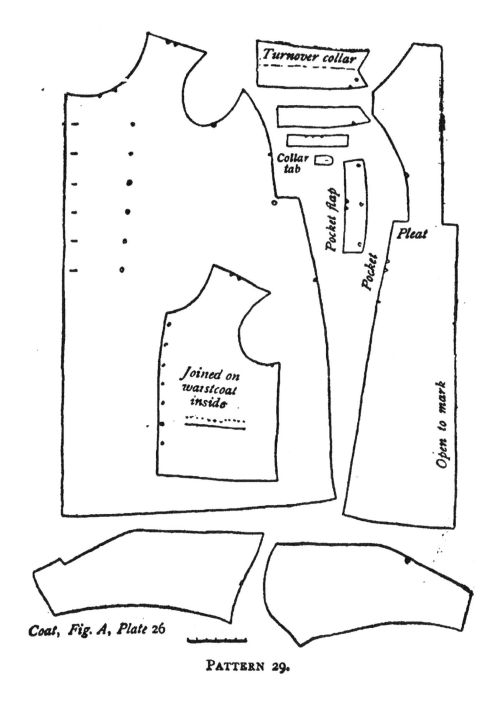

Turnover collar

Collar
tab

Pocket flap

Pocket

Pleat

Open to mark

Joined on
waistcoat
inside

Coat, Fig. A, Plate 26

PATTERN 29.

313

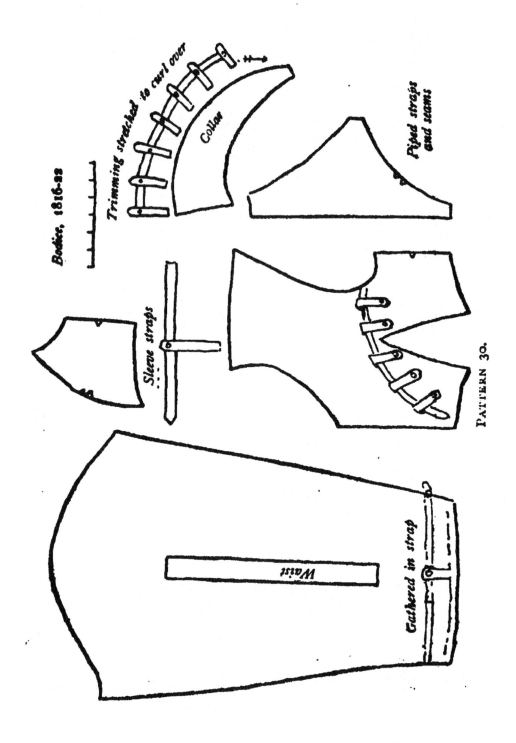

Bodice, 1816-22

Trimming stretched to curl over

Collar

Piped straps and seams

Sleeve straps

Waist

Gathered in strap

PATTERN 30.

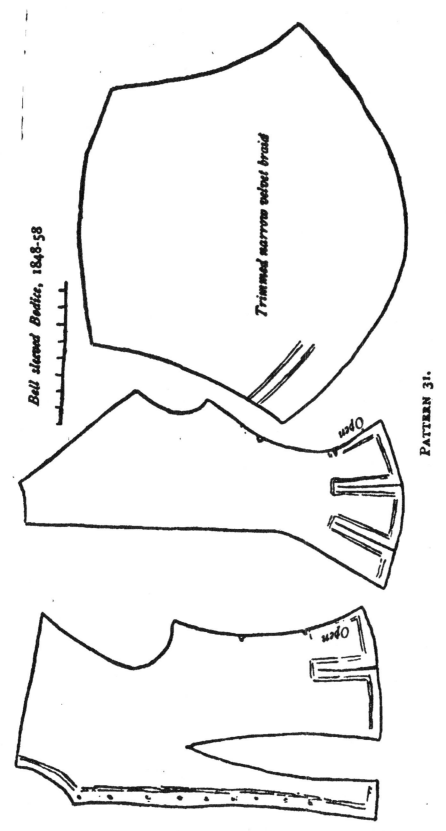

Bell sleeved Bodice, 1848-58

Trimmed narrow velvet braid

Open

Open

PATTERN 31.

315.

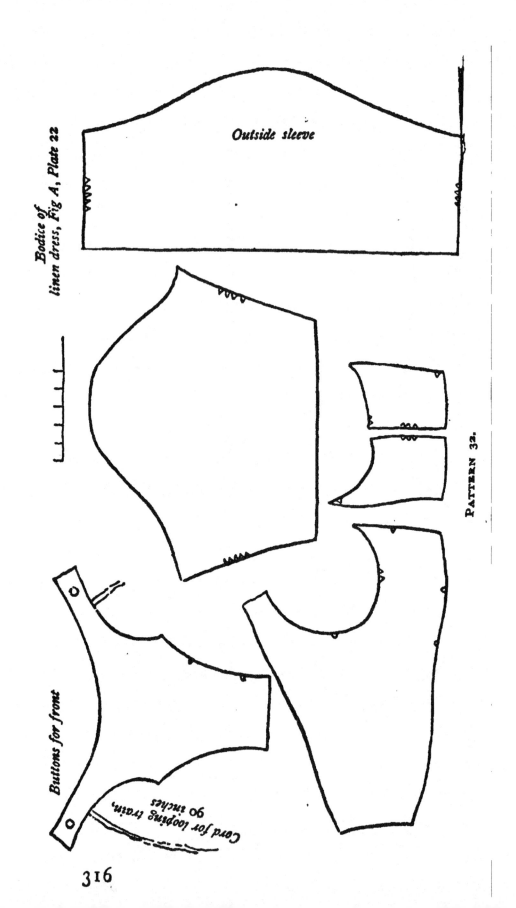

Bodice of
linen dress, Fig A, Plate 22

Outside sleeve

Pattern 32.

Buttons for front

Cord for looping train,
90 inches

316

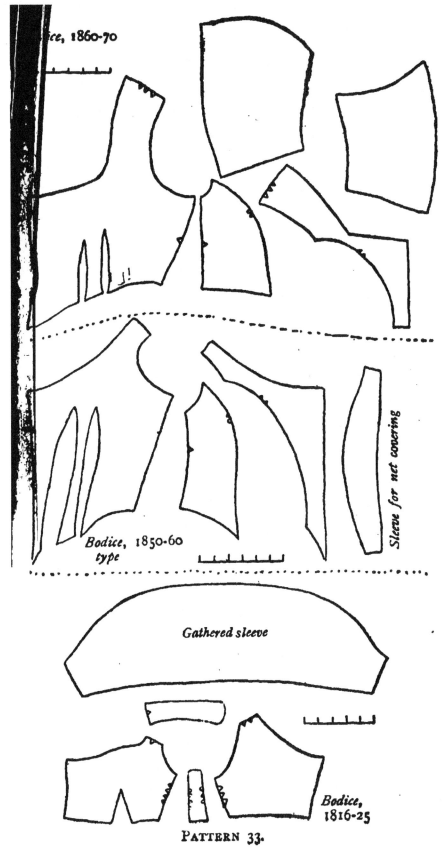

ice, 1860-70

Bodice, 1850-60 type

Sleeve for net covering

Gathered sleeve

Bodice, 1816-25

PATTERN 33.

317

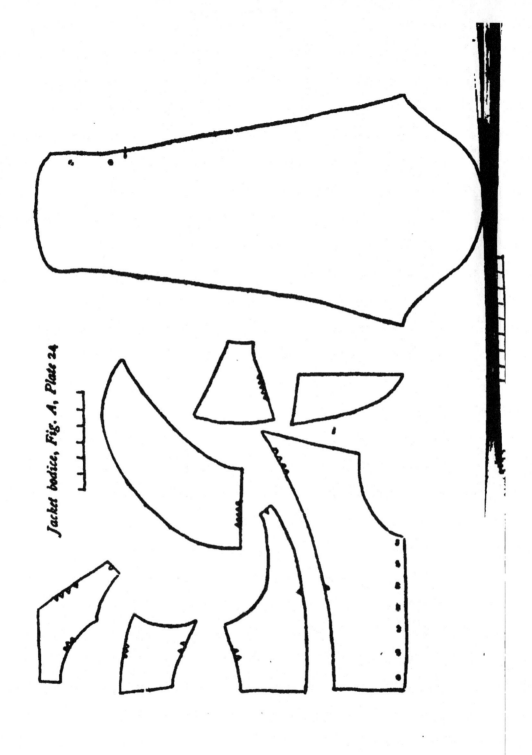

Jacket bodice, Fig. A, Plate 24

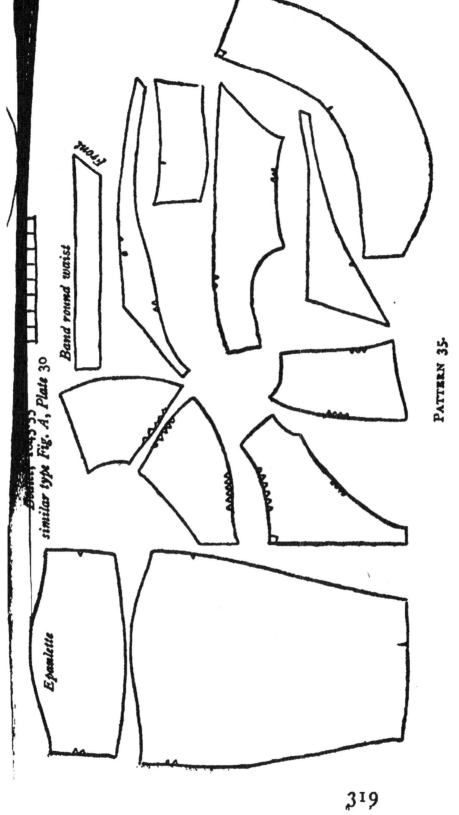

Bodices 1849-55
similar type Fig. A, Plate 30

Band round waist

Front

Epaulette

PATTERN 35.

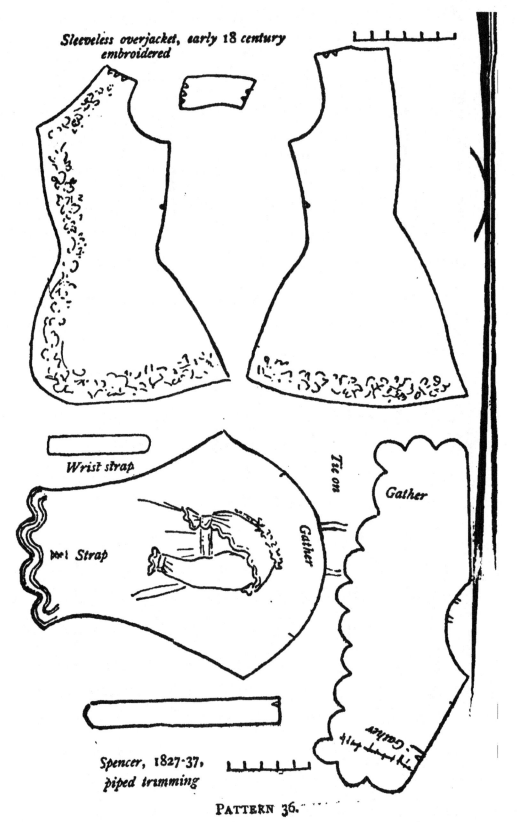

*Sleeveless overjacket, early 18 century
embroidered*

Wrist strap

Part *Strap*

Tie on

Gather

Gather

Gather

*Spencer, 1827-37,
piped trimming*

PATTERN 36.

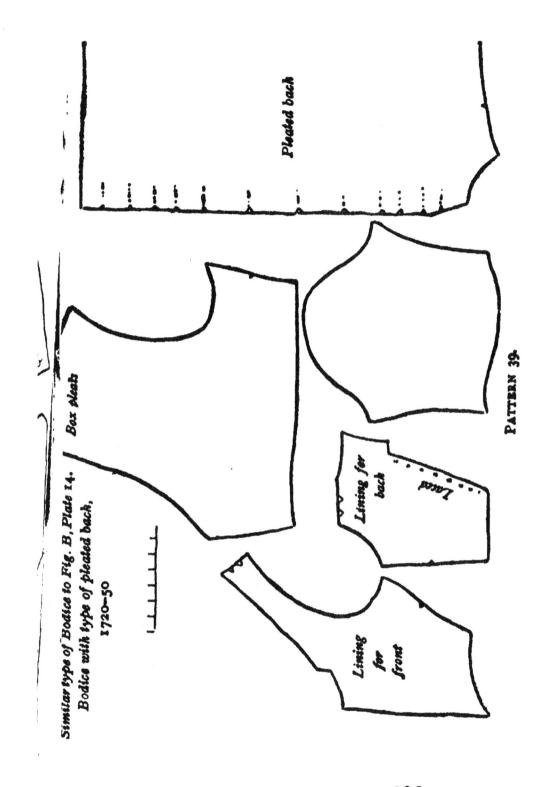

Pleated back

Similar type of Bodice to Fig. B, Plate 14.
Box pleats

Bodice with type of pleated back,
1720–50

Lining for
back

Laced

Lining
for
front

PATTERN 39.

323

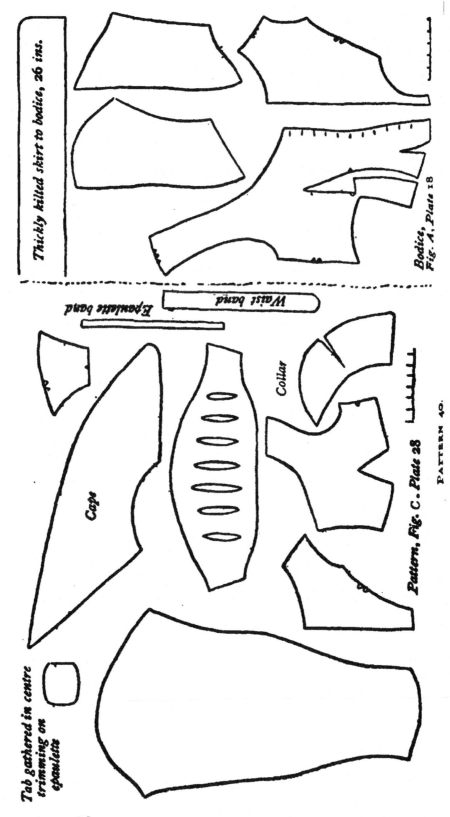

Thickly killed skirt to bodice, 26 ins.

Bodice,
Fig. A, Plate 18

Epaulette band

Waist band

Cape

Collar

Pattern, Fig. C. Plate 28

PATTERN 40.

Tab gathered in centre
trimming on
epaulette

324

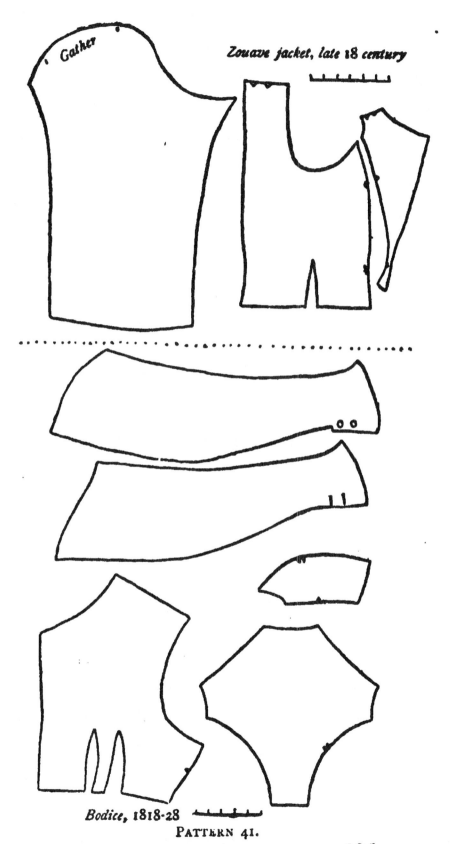

Gather

Zouave jacket, late 18 century

Bodice, 1818-28

PATTERN 41.

325

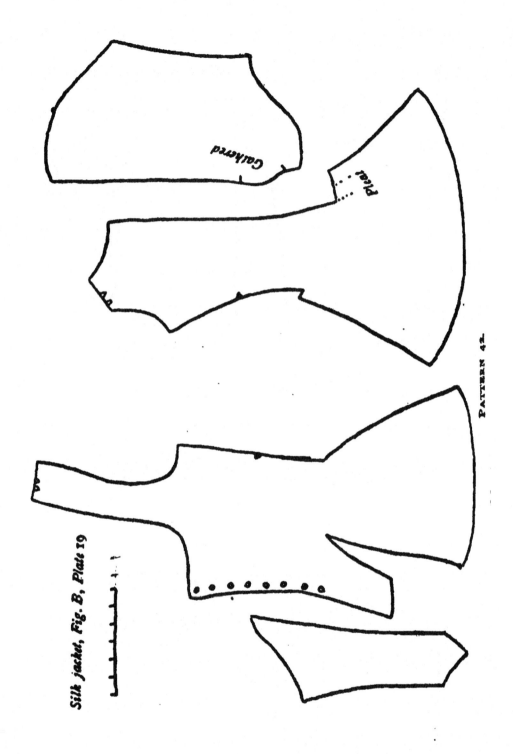

Gathered

Pleat

Silk jacket, Fig. B, Plate 19

PATTERN 42.

326

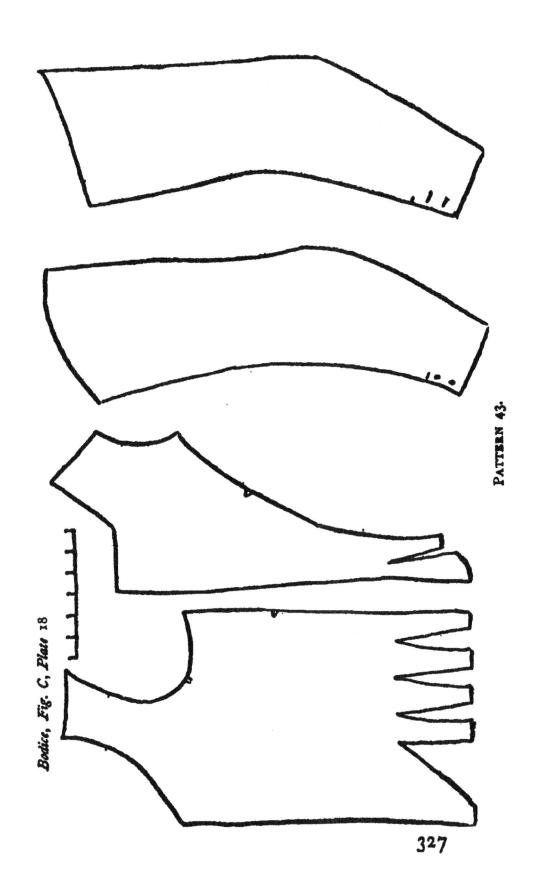

Bodice, Fig. C, Plate 18

PATTERN 43.

327

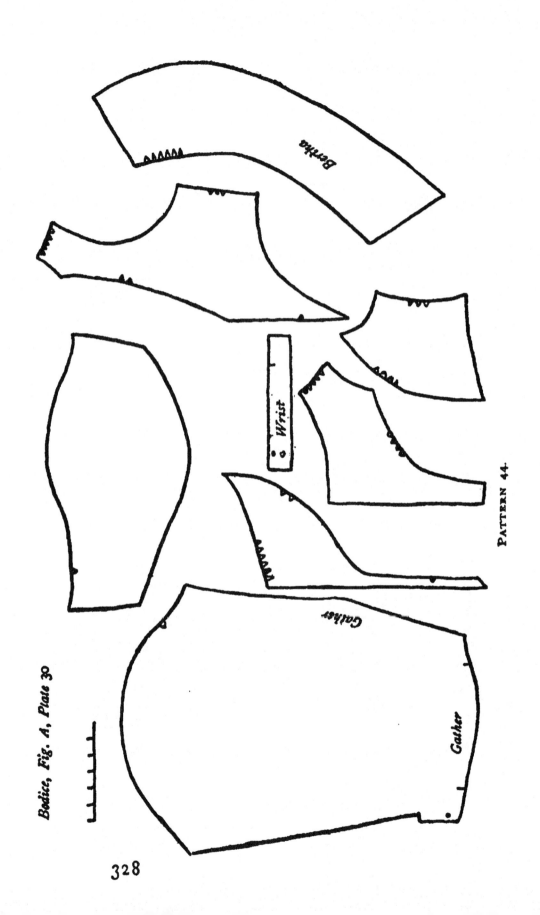

Bertha

Wrist

Gather

Gather

PATTERN 44.

Bodice, Fig. A, Plate 30

328

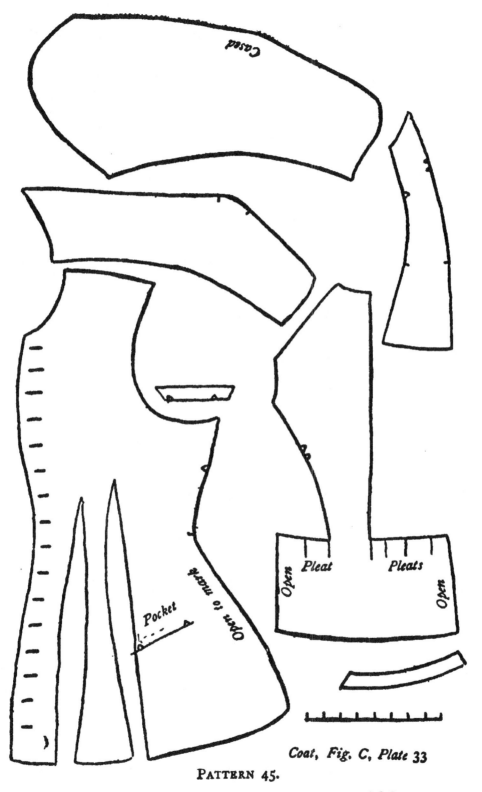

Cased

Open is mark

Pocket

Open   Pleat   Pleats   Open

PATTERN 45.

Coat, Fig. C, Plate 33

329

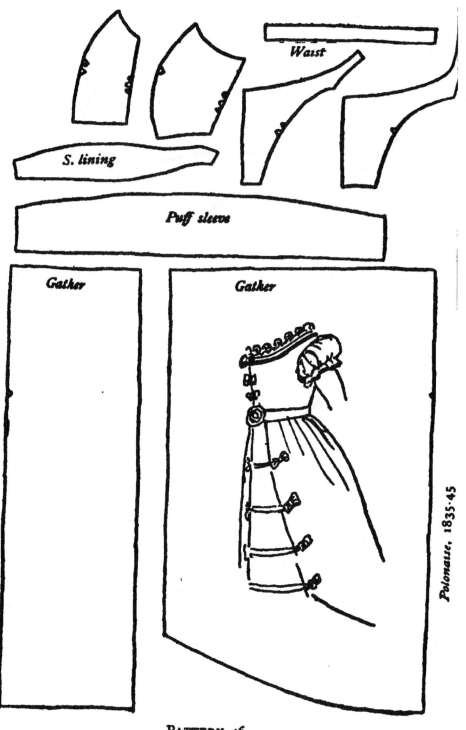

Waist

S. lining

Puff sleeve

Gather

Gather

Polonaise, 1835-45

PATTERN 46.

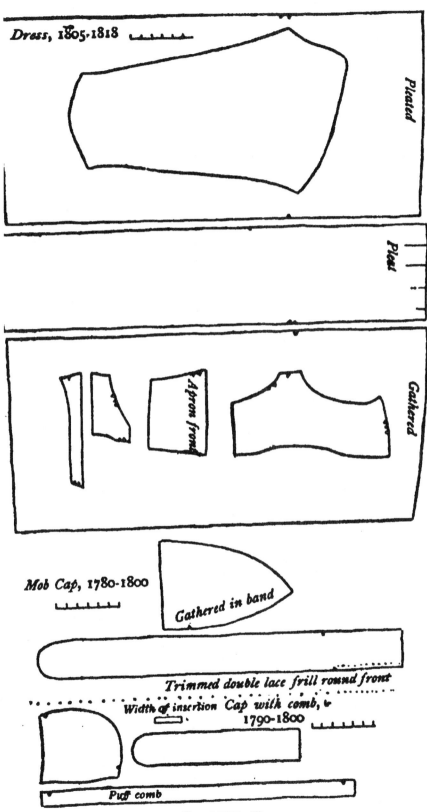

Dress, 1805-1818

Pleated

Pleat

Gathered

Apron front

Mob Cap, 1780-1800

Gathered in band

Trimmed double lace frill round front

Width of insertion Cap with comb, &
1790-1800

Puff comb

PATTERN 47.

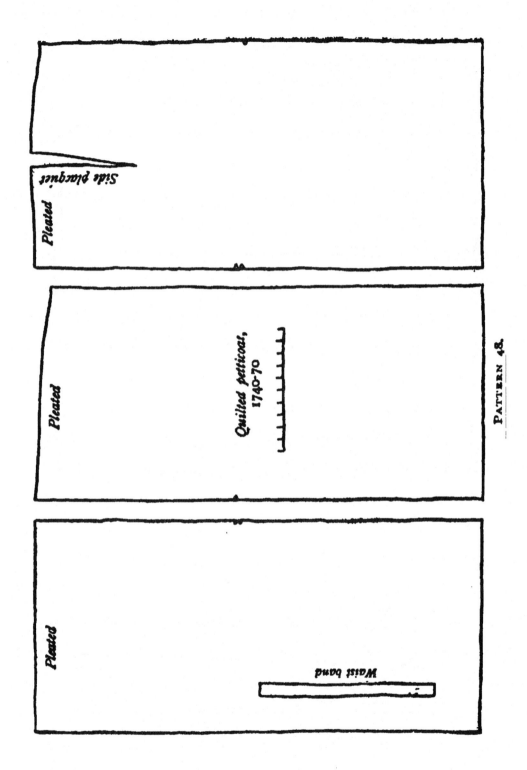

Pleated

Side placquet

Pleated

Quilted petticoat,
1740-70

Pleated

Waist band

PATTERN 48.

332

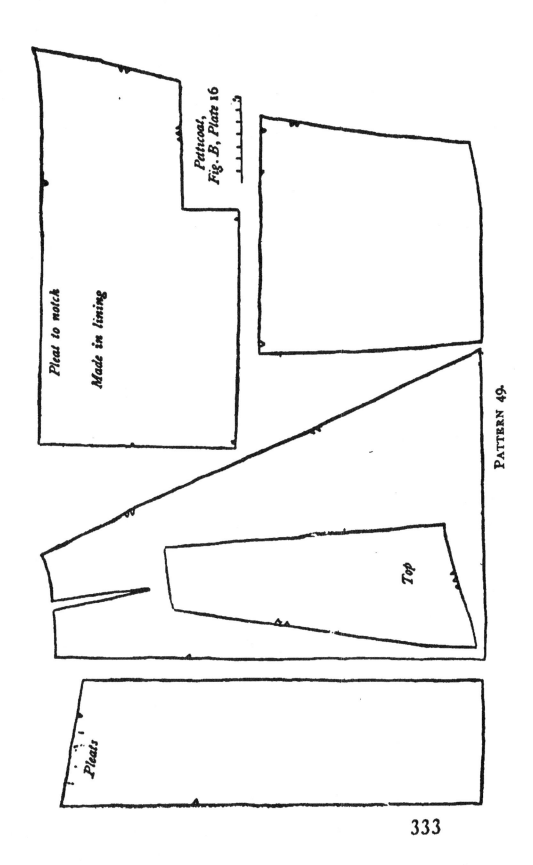

Pleat to notch

Made in lining

Petticoat,
Fig. B, Plate 16

PATTERN 49.

Top

Pleats

333

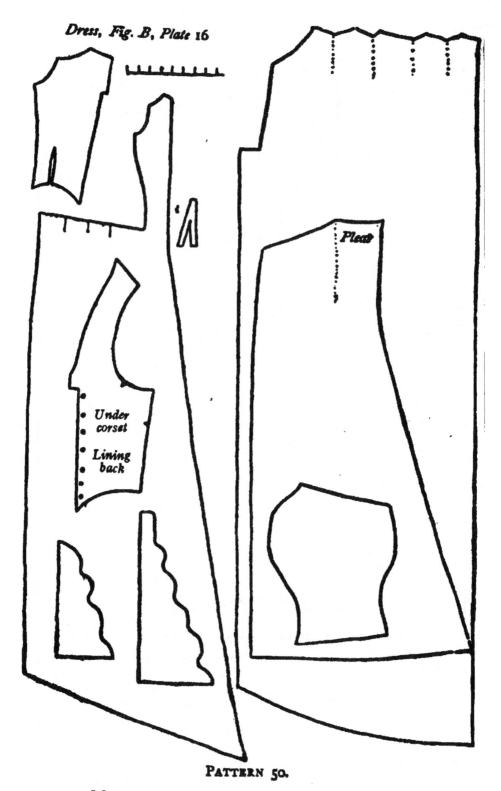

Dress, Fig. B, Plate 16

Under
corset

Lining
back

Pleat

PATTERN 50.

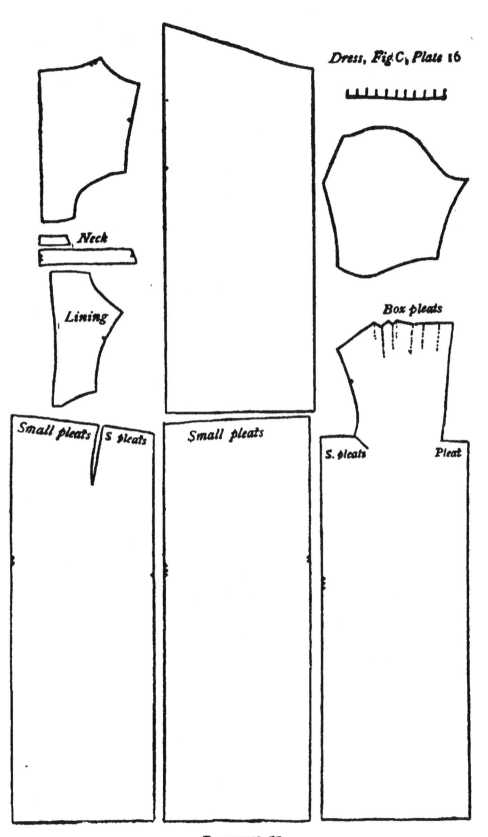

Dress, Fig. C, Plate 16

Neck

Lining

Box pleats

Small pleats   S. pleats   Small pleats   S. pleats   Pleat

PATTERN 51.

335

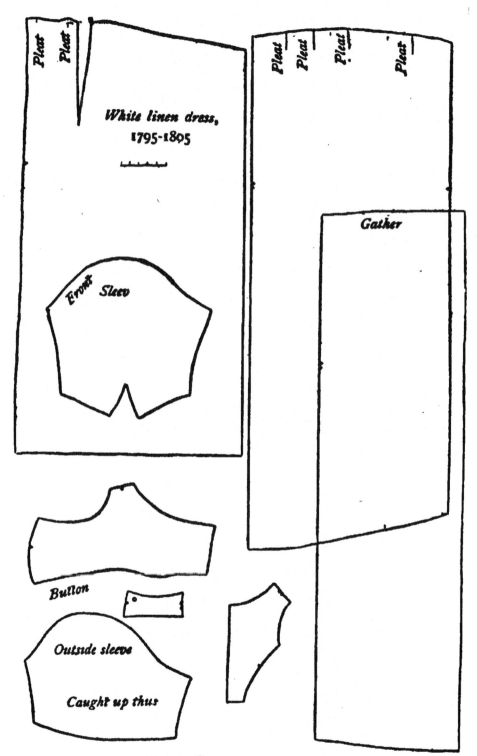

White linen dress,
1795-1805

Pleat Pleat

Pleat Pleat Pleat Pleat

Gather

Front Sleev

Button

Outside sleeve

Caught up thus

PATTERN 52.

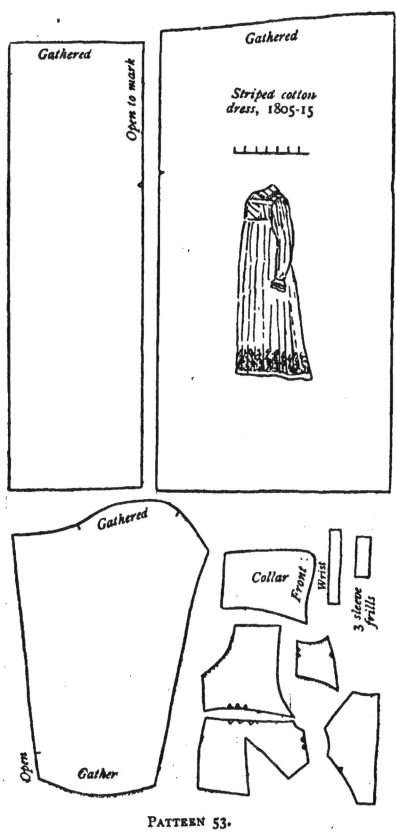

Gathered

Open to mark

Gathered

*Striped cotton
dress, 1805-15*

Gathered

Open

Gather

Collar

Front

Wrist

*3 sleeve
frills*

PATTERN 53.

Y

337

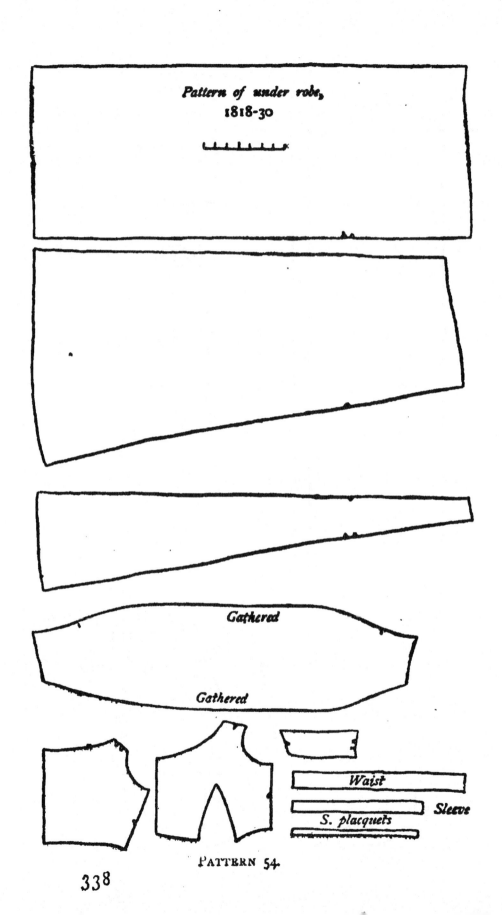

Pattern of under robe,
1818-30

Gathered

Gathered

Waist

Sleeve

S. placquets

PATTERN 54.

338

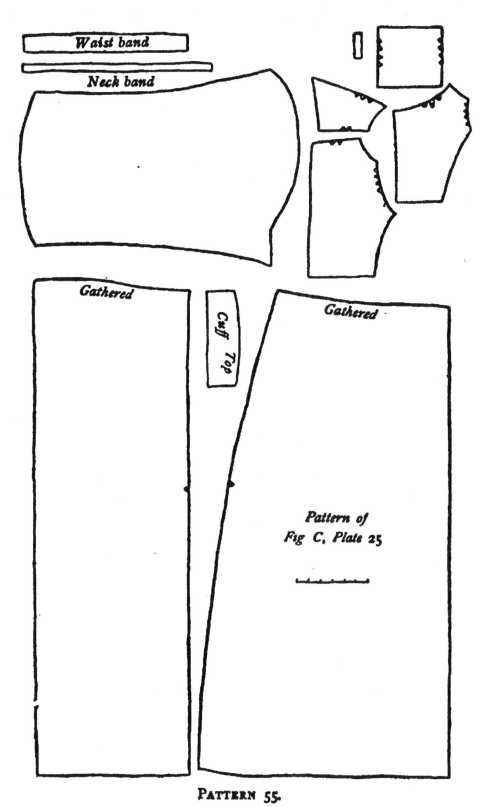

Waist band

Neck band

Gathered

Cuff Top

Gathered

Pattern of
Fig C, Plate 25

PATTERN 55.

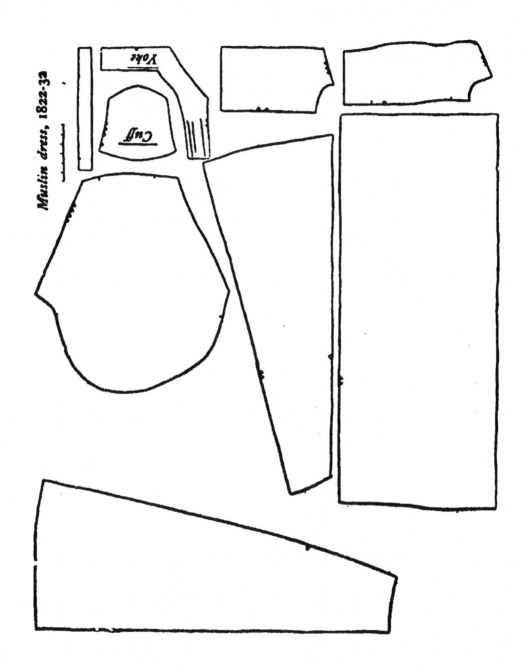

Muslin dress, 1822-32

Yoke

Cuff

340

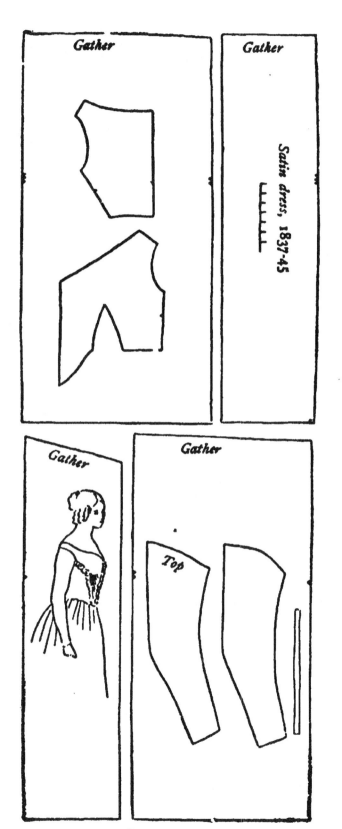

PATTERN 57.

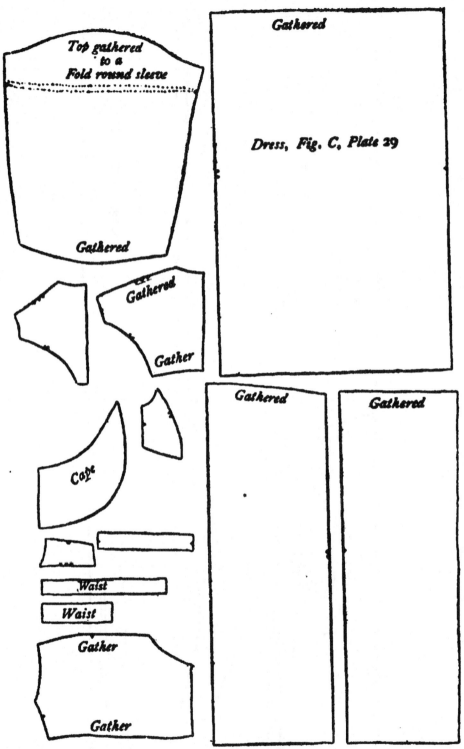

Top gathered
to a
Fold round sleeve

Gathered

Gathered

Dress, Fig. C, Plate 29

Gathered

Gather

Cape

Gathered

Gathered

Waist

Waist

Gather

Gather

PATTERN 58.

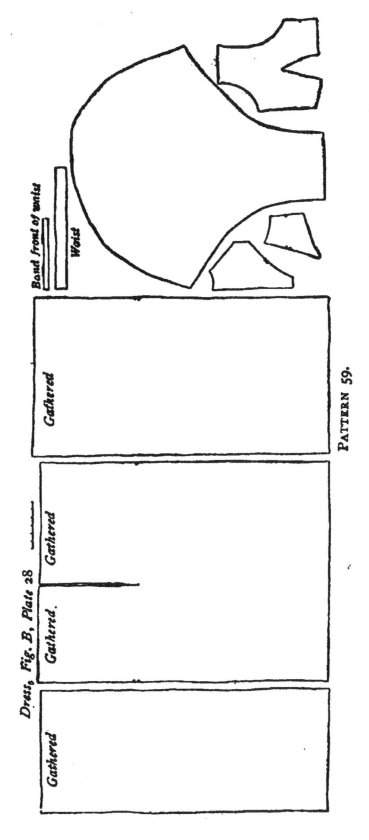

Dress, Fig. B, Plate 28

Gathered

Gathered.

Gathered

Gathered

Gathered

Band front of waist

Waist

PATTERN 59.

343

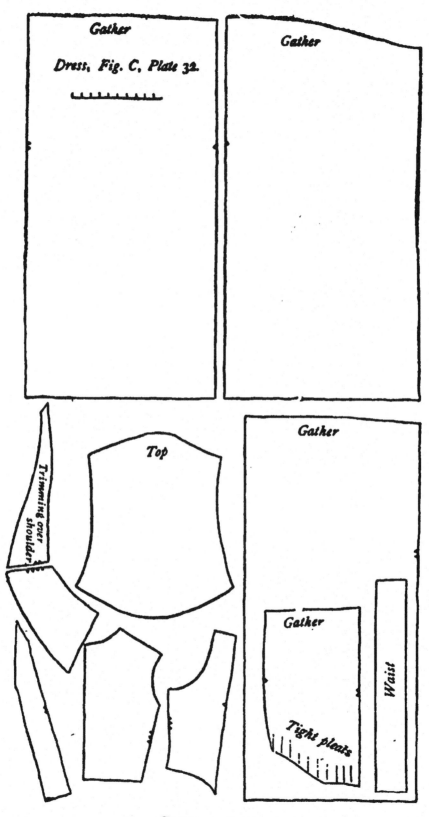

Gather

Dutch, Fig. C, Plate 32.

Gather

Top

Trimming over shoulder

Gather

Gather

Waist

Tight pleats

PATTERN 60.

344

Lady's coat, 1856-70

PATTERN 61.

345

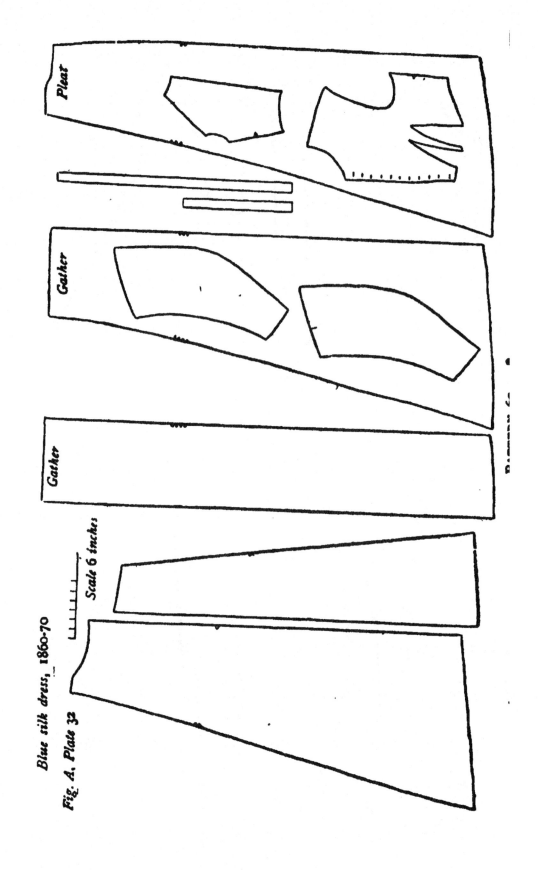

Blue silk dress, 1860-70

Fig. A. Plate 32

Scale 6 inches

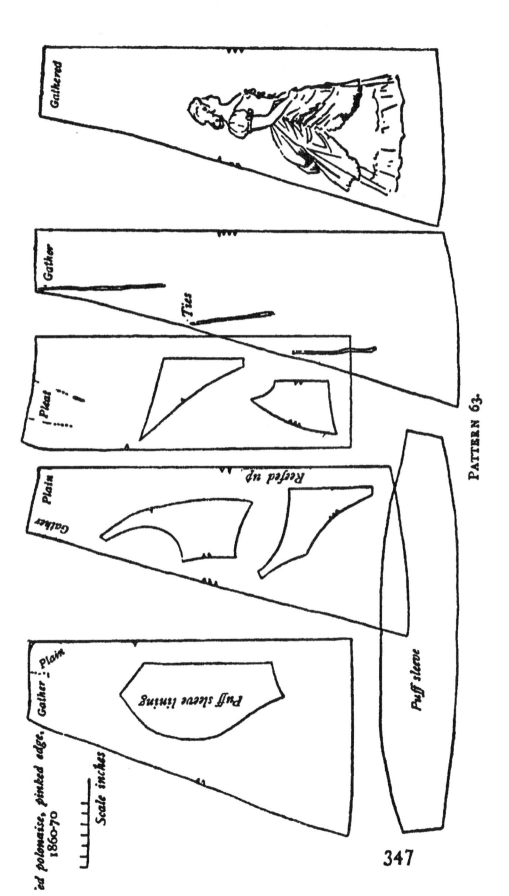

Gathered

Gather

Ties

Pleat

Plain

Reefed up

Gather

Puff sleeve lining

Puff sleeve

...ed polonaise, pinked edge, Gather : Plain
1860-70

Scale inches

PATTERN 63.

347

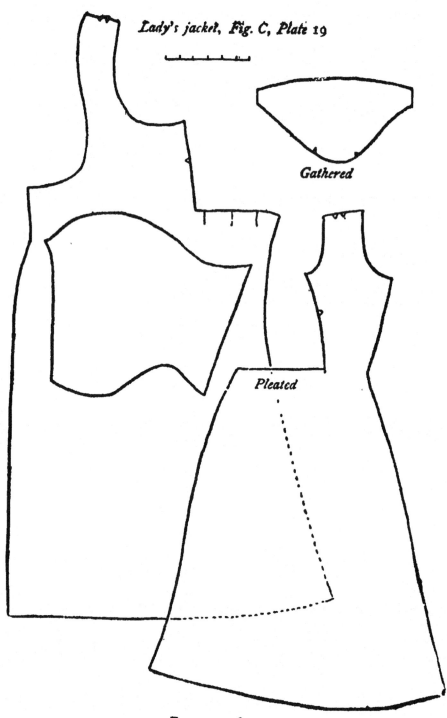

Lady's jacket, Fig. C, Plate 19

Gathered

Pleated

PATTERN 64.

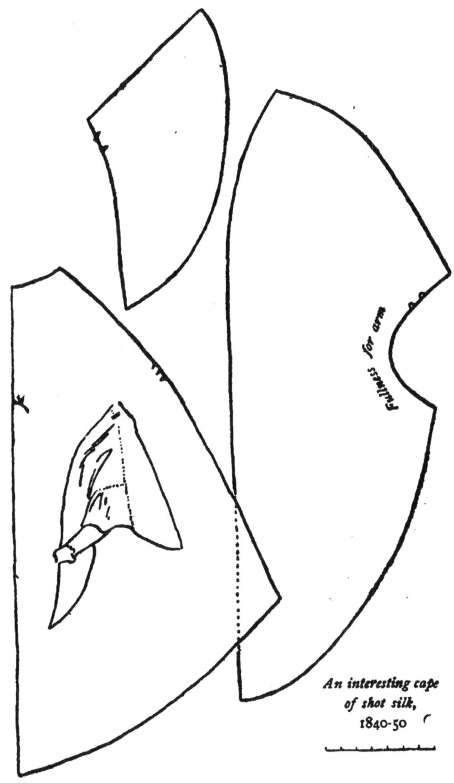

Fullness for arm

An interesting cape
of shot silk,
1840-50

PATTERN 65.

349

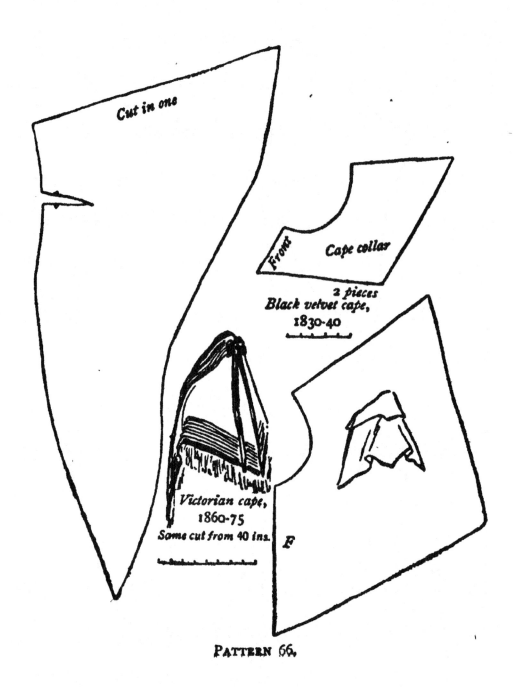

Cut in one

Front Cape collar
2 pieces
Black velvet cape,
1830-40

Victorian cape,
1860-75
Some cut from 40 ins.

F

PATTERN 66.

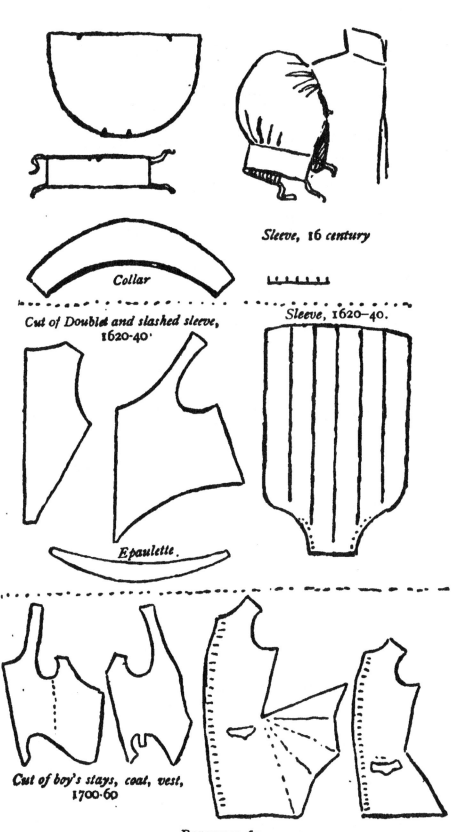

Sleeve, 16 century

Collar

Cut of Doublet and slashed sleeve,
1620-40

Sleeve, 1620-40.

Epaulette.

Cut of boy's stays, coat, vest,
1700-60

PATTERN 67.

351

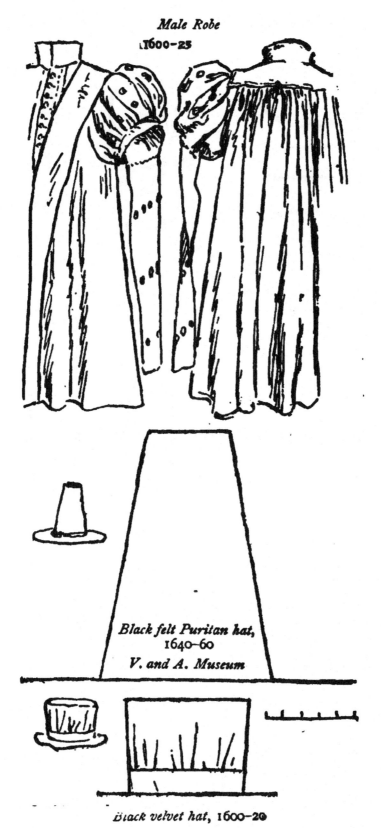

Male Robe
1600-25

Black felt Puritan hat,
1640-60
V. and A. Museum

Black velvet hat, 1600-20

PATTERN 68.

352

DETAILED LIST OF SCALED PATTERNS

Pattern 1, page 285 :—
    Piccadillo, 1580–1630.
    Three caps, 16–17 century.
    Cap of three pieces, 16–17 c.
    Triangular cap, 16–17 c.
    Long cap, 17 c.
    Cap, late 17 c., early 18 c.

Pattern 2, page 286 :—
    4 collars, 17 c.
    Gorget of linen, 17 c.
    2 stocks, 17 and 18 c.
    3 male caps and 1 female, 17 and 18 c.

Pattern 3, page 287 :—
    Ruff, 17 c.
    4 extra linen sleeves, 17 and one 18 c.
    2 caps, female, 17 c.

Pattern 4, page 288 :—
    Front of linen jacket, 16 c.
    Front of linen bodice, Charles I.

Pattern 5, page 289 :—
    Elizabethan jerkin.
    4 stomachers, 17 and 18 c.

z

Detailed
List of
Scaled
Patterns

Pattern 6, page 290 :—
    Set of tabs for male jerkin, 17 c.
    Pattern type, sleeve and bodice front, 1570-1605.
Pattern 7, page 291 :—
    Circular cape, 17 c.
    Cap, female, 1580-1630.
Pattern 8, page 292 :—
    Bodice, Fig. 1, Plate X, James I.
Pattern 9, page 293 :—
    3 corsets and bodice of, Fig. 2, Plate V, 17 c.
Pattern 10, page 294 :—
    Jerkin of white quilted satin, 17 c.
Pattern 11, page 295 :—
    Breeches of same suit.
Pattern 12, page 296 :—
    Cape-coat, 17 c.
Pattern 13, page 297 :—
    Back of bodice, Plate VII, 17 c.
    Shaped cap, male, 17 and 18 c.
Pattern 14, page 298 :—
    2 collars, Charles II.
Pattern 15, page 299 :—
    Jacket, Fig. C, Plate IV, 17 c.
Pattern 16, page 300 :—
    2 sleeve-cuffs, 18 c.
    2 embroidered pockets, 17 and 18 c.
    Hanging sleeve, Fig. C, Plate II, 16-17 c.
    Embroidered bodice fronts, 17-18 c.
Pattern 17, page 301 :—
    Quilted linen corsage, 1660-1715.
    Herald's coat, Fig. A, Plate VII, 16-17 c.
Pattern 18, page 302 :—
    Sleeved waistcoat, 1690-1720.
Pattern 19, page 303 :—
    Sleeved waistcoat and vest, early 18 c.

Pattern 20, page 304 :—
    Breeches, 1660–1720.
Pattern 21, page 305 :—
    Breeches, 18 c.
Pattern 22, page 306 :—
    Breeches, 18 c.
Pattern 23, page 307 :—
    Coat, Fig. *B*, Plate XXVI, 19 c.
Pattern 24, page 308 :—
    Coat, Fig. *B*, Plate XIII, 18 c.
    Corderoy trousers, from 1815.
Pattern 25, page 309 :—
    Coat, late 18 c, Fig. *A*, Plate XV.
    Leather breeches, late 18–19 c.
    Straw hat, 1816–30.
Pattern 26, page 310 :—
    Coat, 1784–94.
Pattern 27, page 311 :—
    Coat, 1830–45.
Pattern 28, page 312 :—
    Buff linen trousers, 1810–40.
Pattern 29, page 313 :—
    Morning coat, Fig. *A*, Plate XXVI, 19 c.
Pattern 30, page 314 :—
    Bodice, 1816–22.
Pattern 31, page 315 :—
    Bell-sleeved bodice, 1848–58.
Pattern 32, page 316 :—
    Bodice of linen dress, Fig. *A*, Plate XXII, about
      1800.
Pattern 33, page 317 :—
    Bodice, 1860–70.
    Bodice, 1850–60.
    Bodice, 1816–25.
Pattern 34, page 318 :—
    Jacket bodice, Fig. *A*, Plate XXIV, about 1800.

Detailed
List of
Scaled
Patterns

Pattern 35, page 319 :—
 Bodice, similar type, Fig. *A*, Plate XXX,
  1845–55.
Pattern 36, page 320 :—
 Sleeveless overjacket, early 18 c.
 Spencer, 1827–37.
Pattern 37, page 321 :—
 Bodice, 1812–18.
Pattern 38, page 322 :—
 Corset pattern, 18 c.
 Bodice of Fig. *A*, Plate XIV, 18 c.
Pattern 39, page 323 :—
 Bodice with type of pleated sack back, 1720–50.
Pattern 40, page 324 :—
 Bodice, Fig. *C*, Plate XXVIII, 19 c.
 Bodice, Fig. *A*, Plate XVIII, 18 c.
Pattern 41, page 325 :—
 Zouave jacket, late 18 c.
 Bodice, 1818–28.
Pattern 42, page 326 :—
 Silk jacket, Fig. *B*, Plate XIX, 18 c.
Pattern 43, page 327 :—
 Bodice, Fig. *C*, Plate XVIII, 18 c.
Pattern 44, page 328 :—
 Bodice, Fig. *A*, Plate XXX, 19 c.
Pattern 45, page 329 :—
 Lady's coat, Fig. *C*, Plate XXXIII.
Pattern 46, Page 330 :—
 Polonaise dress, 1835–45.
Pattern 47, page 331 :—
 Dress, 1805–18.
 Mob cap, 1780–1800.
 Cap with comb top, 1790–1800.
Pattern 48, page 332 :—
 Quilted petticoat, 18 c.
Pattern 49, page 333 :—
 Petticoat, Fig. *B*, Plate XVI, 18 c.

Pattern 50, page 334 :—
    Dress, Fig. *B*, Plate XVI.
Pattern 51, page 335 :—
    Dress, Fig. *C*, Plate XVI.
Pattern 52, page 336 :—
    White linen dress, 1795–1800.
Pattern 53, page 337 :—
    Striped cotton dress, 1805–15.
Pattern 54, page 338 :—
    Pattern of under robe, 1818–30.
Pattern 55, page 339 :—
    Dress, Fig. *G*, Plate XXV.
Pattern 56, page 340 :—
    Muslin dress, 1822–32.
Pattern 57, page 341 :—
    Satin dress, 1837–47.
Pattern 58, page 342 :—
    Dress, Fig. *G*, Plate XXIX.
Pattern 59, page 343 :—
    Dress, Fig. *B*, Plate XXVIII.
Pattern 60, page 344 :—
    Dress, Fig. *C*, Plate XXXII.
Pattern 61, page 345 :—
    Lady's coat, 1856–70.
Pattern 62, page 346 :—
    Silk dress, Fig. *A*, Plate XXXII, 1860–70.
Pattern 63, page 347 :—
    Reefed polonaise, 1860–70.
Pattern 64, page 348 :—
    Lady's jacket, Fig. *C*, Plate XIX, 18 c.
Pattern 65, page 349 :—
    Cape, 1840–50.
Pattern 66, page 350 :—
    Cape, 1860–75.
    Cape, 1830–40.

Detailed List of Scaled Patterns

Pattern 67, page 351 :—
    Upper sleeve and collar, 16 c.
    Bodice with slashed sleeve, 1620–40.
    Boy's stays, coat, and vest, 1700–60.
Pattern 68, page 352 :—
    Male robe, 1600–25.
    Puritan hat, 1640–60.
    Black velvet hat, 1600–20.

INDEX

APRONS—
  17 century, 186, 280
  18 c., 192, 198, 206

BAGS, 193, 262, 272
Bertha, 238, 252
Bouquet Holder, 262
Breeches—
  Mediæval, 54
  16 c., 122, 132
  17 c., 152, 164, 281
  19 c., 248, 256, 264
Bustle, 226

CALASH, 217
Capes—
  16 c., 132, 279
  17 c., 184
  19 c., 244, 262, 264, 274, 281
Chain Ornaments—
  to 15 c., 62, 72
  16 c., 110, 124
Cloaks—
  to 15 c., 54, 70
  17 c., 152, 164, 176, 180, 279
  18 c., 222
Collars—
  16 c., 112, 128, 129, 139, 278

Collars (cont.)—
  17 c., 145, 158, 160, 172 174
  19 c., 244, 246
Corsets—
  to 15 c., 62, 66
  16 c., 110, 116, 138
  17 c., 158, 169, 172
  18 c., 211, 278
  19 c., 250
Crinolines, 270, 278

DECORATIVE Styles—
  Black-stitch work, 122, 129
  Braided, 110, 111, 132, 142, 143, 144, 145, 146, 182, 188, 200, 238, 244, 272
  Button, 110, 143, 144, 146, 182, 210
  Laced, 70, 88, 92, 110, 116
  Piped, 238, 244
  Pleated, 111, 140
  Pricked, } 111, 140, 142,
  Punched, } 152
  Puffed, 88, 92, 110, 116, 118, 122, 129, 142, 146, 150, 180, 260
  Purfled, 145, 164, 190

359

Index

Decorative Styles (*cont.*)—
    Ribbon, 145, 172, 176, 178, 191, 253
    Serrated or shaped edging, 72, 96, 110, 146, 191, 214, 252
    Slashing, 92, 111, 112, 113, 116, 118, 122, 140, 142, 145, 152, 158, 164
    Straw-work, 111, 191
    Tassel, 238
    Tinsel, 237
    Tulle, 238
Doublets, 132, 139
Dress—
    Prehistoric, female, 40; male, 41
    to 10 c., female, 45, 46, 48; male, 52, 54
    10 to 15 c., female, 62, 66, 68, 70; male, 76, 78, 80
    15 c., female, 84, 88, 92; male, 92, 100, 104, 108
    16 c., 278, 279, 281. Henry VIII, female, 113, 116; male, 118, 122. Ed. VI and Mary, female, 124, 128; male, 129, 132. Eliz., female, 133, 136, 138; male, 139, 281
    17 c., James I, female, 147, 150; male, 152, 154. Chas. I, female, 158; male, 160, 164, 168. Commonwealth, female and male, 168, 169. Chas. II, female, 169, 172; male, 174, 176. James II, female, 178, 180; male, 182. William and Mary, female, 184, 185; male, 186, 188. Anne, female, 196;

Dress (*cont.*)—
    male, 200. George I, female, 206; male, 210
    18 c., George II, female, 211; male, 214. George III to 1800, female, 217, 222, 224, 226, 230; male, 232, 234
    19 c., George III (*continued*), female, 244, 247; male, 247. George IV, female, 250; male, 254. William IV, female, 260; male, 263. Victorian, female, 268; male, 274. Note also page 39
Drill petticoat, 238

Ear-rings, 62—72
Epaulets—
    16 c., 128, 129, 136
    17 c., 143, 152, 280, 281
    19 c., 250

Fans—
    16 c., 129, 138
    18 c., 193, 230
    19 c., 240, 253, 262
Farthingale, 111, 136
Foot-wear—
    to the end of 14 c., 44, 48, 56, 70, 80, 82, 92
    15 c., 108
    16 c., Henry VIII, 16, 122; Ed. VI and Mary, 128, 132; Elizabeth, 138, 140
    17 c., James I, 150, 154; Chas. I, 158, 164; Commonwealth, 168; Chas. II, 172, 176; James II, 180, 184; William and Mary, 186, 188
    18 c., 193; Anne, 198, 201; George I, 207, 210;

Foot-wear (*cont.*)—
George II, 214, 216 ;
George III to 1800, 230,
234
19 c., George III, 246, 248 ;
George IV, 253, 258 ;
William IV, 262, 264 ;
Victoria, 272, 275

GIRDLES—
to 15 c., 68, 78, 92
16 c., 116
Gloves—
16 c., 116, 129, 138
17 c., 168, 172
18 c., 193, 201, 214, 226

HEAD-DRESS—
Prehistoric, female, 40 ;
male, 42
to 10 c., female, 45 ; male,
49
10 to 15 c., female, 57 ;
male, 71
15 c., female, 84 ; male,
92
16 c., Henry VIII, female,
113 ; male, 118. Ed.
VI and Mary, female,
124 ; male, 129. Eliz.,
female, 133 ; male, 138
17 c., James I, female,
147 ; male, 150. Chas.
I, female, 154 ; male,
160. Commonwealth,
168. Chas. II, female,
169 ; male, 174. James
II, female, 178 ; male,
180. William and Mary,
female, 184 ; male, 186
18 c., Anne, female, 193 ;
male, 198. George I,
female, 201 ; male, 207.
George II, female, 211 ;

Head-dress (*cont.*)—
male, 214. George III,
female, 217, 241 ; male,
231, 246. George IV,
female, 248 ; male, 254.
William IV, female,
258 ; male, 263. Vic-
toria, female, 264 ; male,
273
Heraldic fashion, 66, 71,
109, 132
Hoop skirts—
16 c., 116, 128, 136
17 c., 147, 185
18 c., 222

JACKETS—
to 15 c., 66, 68, 88, 100
16 c., 112, 182
17 c., 143
18 c., 224, 226
19 c., 270

LAPETS, 184, 193, 206, 239

MACCARONI fashion, 214
Mantles, 262, 271
Masks, 186
Muffs, 160, 172, 180, 186,
189, 193, 201, 230, 253

NECK-WEAR, 174, 182, 186,
200, 207, 232, 246, 250,
254, 263, 275

OVERCOATS, 232, 254, 274

PANNIERS, 211, 222
Parasols, 230, 234, 244, 272
Patterns scaled, 276
Pelisses, 244, 250, 262
Plates (collotypes), frontis-
piece, 39, 42, 55, 58, 71,
74, 87, 90, 103, 106, 119

Index

Plates (*cont.*)—
122, 135, 138, 151, 154,
167, 170, 183, 186, 199,
202, 215, 218, 231, 234,
247, 250, 259, 263, 266,
270, 279, 282
Pockets, 192, 224
Polonaise, 238, 262
Purses, 236, 240, 246

Quilting, 111, 128, 146, 172,
192, 198, 211, 222, 278

Ruffs, 112, 118, 128, 129,
133, 136, 139, 143, 147,
158, 160, 172, 250, 280

Sackback (or Watteau) dress,
136, 185, 191, 196, 206,
211, 222
Sashes, 168, 182, 279
Sequins, 112
Shawls, 272
Spats, 273
Spencers, 244, 250
Sticks, 181, 188, 201, 211,
214, 226, 234
Stockings, 138, 140, 154, 168,
182, 184, 189, 201, 210,
216, 234, 270
Stomachers, 66, 112, 136,
142, 144, 146, 147, 154,
158, 172, 178, 184, 196
207, 278

Printed by Spottiswoode, Ballantyne & Co. Ltd.
Colchester, London & Eton, England

DRESSMAKING

SIMPLE DRESSMAKING. By ETHEL R. HAMBRIDGE, *Art Teachers' Certificate,* *etc.* In foolscap 4to, cloth, 200 pp., with 750 plates and black-and-white diagrams. 7s. 6d. net.

This book deals exhaustively with the various stitches and fastenings used in Dressmaking and their applications, Pressing, Making-up Processes, Taking Measurements, Cutting-out; and also contains some notes on Fitting.

Simplicity and completeness have been the dual purpose of the Author, and her systematic treatment of the subject, aided by her remarkable gift of lucid explanation, and her unique practical experience, has produced a valuable contribution to the literature of Domestic Science.

DRESS CUTTING AND MAKING. For the Classroom, Workroom, and Home. By **EMILY WALLBANK,** *Head of the Needlework and Dressmaking Department, National Training School of Cookery,* and **MARIAN WALLBANK.** In foolscap 4to, cloth, 271 pp., with 265 diagrams and illustrations. 6s. net.

The object of this work will be realized in some degree if it helps the practical reader so to mobilize her knowledge of underlying causes that she is able to produce any desired effect in the cut and fashion of a garment.

SIR ISAAC PITMAN & SONS, LIMITED
1 AMEN CORNER, LONDON, E.C. 4.

EMBROIDERY

AN EMBROIDERY PATTERN BOOK. By MARY E. WARING. With a Foreword by Professor W. R. LETHABY, *Royal College of Art*. In cloth gilt, 170 pp., 2 coloured plates, with 84 full-page black-and-white diagrams. 8*s*. 6*d*. net.

"Designing of this sort is no mystery that requires 'genius'; it is of the same kind as planting a garden border. . . . Most embroideresses, who will begin by adapting the elements given in this Pattern Book, and gain interest and confidence in so doing, will go forward insensibly to varying the elements themselves, and to taking flowers and animals direct from Nature. This . . . is the work of a highly competent designer of embroidery, and I heartily recommend it."—W. R. LETHABY in the Foreword.

EMBROIDERY & DESIGN. By JOAN H. DREW. In foolscap 4to, cloth, about 115 pp., with 82 black-and-white illustrations and designs. 5*s*. net.

The writer endeavours to arouse in her readers a desire for better designs, and greater individuality and thought in the home embroidery of to-day. The difference between decorative and undecorative work is clearly explained with the aid of many illustrations, and these are of the right size for tracing and working.

SIR ISAAC PITMAN & SONS, LIMITED

ART

THE ART OF PAINTING IN PASTEL.
By J. LITTLEJOHNS, R.B.A., and L.
RICHMOND, R.A. With a frontispiece and
foreword by FRANK BRANGWYN, R.A.
With 40 beautiful full-page coloured plates and
15 other illustrations. In demy 4to, cloth gilt.
15s. net.

Extract from *The Connoisseur* :

"The beautiful volume may quicken public interest in the
method. The 40 plates in colour afford a fine series of examples
of the resources of the medium and the best methods of ex-
ploiting them."

DRAWING AND DESIGN. A School
Course in Composition. By S A M U E L
CLEGG, *Headmaster of the County Secondary
School, Long Eaton, Derbyshire*, with a foreword
by WILLIAM ROTHENSTEIN, *Professor
of Civic Art, Sheffield University*. 10 in. by
7¼ in. 12s. 6d. net.

A feature of the book is the inclusion of plates printed
by scholars from wood-blocks of their own making and
designing. It also contains good sections on lettering
and pen and ink drawing, as well as on pencil work,
colour work, etc.

SIR ISAAC PITMAN & SONS, LIMITED

CPSIA information can be obtained at www.ICGtesting.com
Printed in the USA
BVOW09s0958090215

386954BV00019B/264/P